A BANTAM PATHFINDER EDITION

From Plymouth Rock to Little Rock
to Memphis . . .

THE NEGRO PILGRIMAGE IN AMERICA

has been a long and arduous one—
often marked by tragedy, but always
sustained by spirit. Here is the story of a
march that began almost 400 years
ago—the true tales of individual men and
women, as well as a proud panorama
of a people who enriched American
culture and life.

Books by C. Eric Lincoln

THE BLACK MUSLIMS IN AMERICA
MY FACE IS BLACK
SOUNDS OF THE STRUGGLE
IS ANYBODY LISTENING TO BLACK AMERICA?
A PICTORIAL HISTORY OF THE NEGRO IN AMERICA
    (with Langston Hughes and Milton Meltzer)
A PROFILE OF MARTIN LUTHER KING
THE NEGRO PILGRIMAGE IN AMERICA

Published by Bantam Books, Inc.

BANTAM PATHFINDER EDITIONS

Bantam Pathfinder Editions provide the best in
fiction and nonfiction in a wide variety of
subject areas. They include novels by classic
and contemporary writers; vivid, accurate
histories and biographies; authoritative works
in the sciences; collections of short
stories, plays and poetry.

Bantam Pathfinder Editions are carefully
selected and approved. They are durably bound,
printed on specially selected high-quality paper,
and presented in a new and handsome format.

THE NEGRO PILGRIMAGE IN AMERICA

THE COMING OF AGE OF THE BLACKAMERICANS

BY C. ERIC LINCOLN

**Professor of Sociology and Religion,
Union Theological Seminary**

BANTAM BOOKS

BANTAM PATHFINDER EDITIONS
NEW YORK / TORONTO / LONDON

RLI: $\dfrac{\text{VLM } 9.0}{\text{IL } 8.12}$

THE NEGRO PILGRIMAGE IN AMERICA
A Bantam Pathfinder Book / published November 1967
2nd printing....November 1967   4th printing.........July 1968
3rd printing........April 1968   5th printing....September 1968
Revised Bantam Pathfinder edition published October 1969

Library of Congress Catalog Card Number: 67-28881

*Copyright © 1967, 1969 by Anti-Defamation League of
B'nai B'rith*
*This book may not be reproduced in whole or in part, by
mimeograph or any other means, without permission.
For information address: Bantam Books, Inc.*

Published simultaneously in the United States and Canada

*Bantam Books are published by Bantam Books, Inc., a National
General company. Its trade-mark, consisting of the words "Bantam
Books" and the portrayal of a bantam, is registered in the United
States Patent Office and in other countries Marca Registrada.
Bantam Books, Inc., 666 Fifth Avenue, New York, N.Y. 10019.*

PRINTED IN THE UNITED STATES OF AMERICA

*Dedicated
to Lyman V. Cady
and Albert Victor Danielsen*

Acknowledgment

The editors are indebted to Mr. Greg Harris for his generous assistance in preparing this book. We would also like to express our appreciation to the following institutions and organizations for their cooperation in the selection of photographs: the AFL-CIO, CORE, NAACP, the Department of Photography at the Museum of Modern Art, the staff of the Picture Collection at the New York Public Library, and the National Urban League. Special thanks are due Ernest Kaiser of the Schomburg Collection of the New York Public Library, and William Katz who released photographs from his personal collection.

Contents

We have come
Over a way that with tears has been watered
We have come
Treading a path through the blood of the slaughtered
Out of the gloomy past
'Til now we stand at last
Where the white gleam of our bright star
Is cast.

JAMES WELDON JOHNSON

If the American Negro is to be seen in proper perspective as a part of contemporary American society, it is important to know something of his origins and the peculiar set of circumstances which has marked his pilgrimage from bondsman to responsible citizen. And, if he is ever to be appreciated as an American, the Negro must be seen in the full context of America's growth and development. American history is *his* history, and his history is part of America's. Any account of what happened in America which does not fully reflect the Negro's presence and activities is to that degree unfaithful to reality.

The Negro pilgrimage begins in Africa, the land of the rootstock of America's Negroes. From West Africa they came as slaves: from Guinea, from Calabar, from Gambia and Angola, from a hundred tribes and a thousand villages. Down to the waiting ships out of Lisbon and Cadiz, London and Liverpool, Newport and Boston, they marched chained together in coffles.

The Europeans who came to America came in search of a new and more complete freedom; the Africans came because the last vestige of their freedom had been taken away. The Europeans came in search of new ways to exploit the full potential of their humanity; the Africans came under conditions which denied even their basic humanity. The children of West Africa and the sons and daughters of Europe were destined for separate roles in the making of America. For the white Europeans, America was to be a land of the free, where the self-evident truths of human equality were to be sufficient ground for individual liberty and universal justice. For the black African, America was to mean two hundred and fifty years of slavery. After that would come the belated discovery that even with freedom there were social and moral factors which would qualify that freedom for yet another hundred years, and more.

It was of no significance to colonial America that many of the Africans she held as slaves came directly from, or were descendants of cultures which were by any objective standards highly developed. Unfortunately, the slave period in America was a period of racial and cultural provincialism oblivious to any values not consistent with or comforming to those prevailing in Western Europe. The African political, artistic, economic, religious and linguistic experience was not European, and was thus judged to be of no consequence for the New World which was organized in terms of the European experience. Africans were prohibited from practicing and developing their art, their language, their religion, their family life— and for want of appreciation and practice, whatever was distinctively African soon died out in America.

We cannot hope to resurrect a substantial representation of the African past in a work of this limited scope. But we can hope to offer a look at some characteristic forms of African cultural experience. Since most of the slaves sold in America came from West Africa, we may justifiably restrict our inquiry to that area, although to treat the whole of West Africa as a single culture does further violence to the whole matter of African identity. One of the historic problems of the slaves and their descendants was that in the practical matter of grouping slaves for sale or for work, the slavemaster paid no attention to cultural or linguistic differences. The suffering of the slave was thereby made more acute because his sense of personal identity was shattered. Even among other blacks, he could not always communicate.

Over eight hundred indigenous languages are spoken on the African continent. To this day, in the modern state of Nigeria alone, two hundred languages are used. For the African, the spoken language is his history, his newspaper, his link to a tribe. In the local market places, oral literature developed into an elaborate tradition. Some of our American Negro folklore has its roots in this oral tradition which came with the slaves from Africa.

Music and dancing also play important roles in African life, both as part of religious ceremonials and as a recreational activity. African music is complex in scale and rhythm, with arrangements usually featuring responsive choral patterns. Instrumentation makes great use of the drum, although woodwind instruments are also widely used.

In addition to a highly developed oral literature and music, West Africans are noted for their original sculpture. The wood carvings, bronzes, stone carvings and ivory work of the sixteenth and seventeenth centuries have had a strong influence on modern Western art. Africans also developed a highly intricate system of metal work, utilizing the continent's vast mineral ore deposits.

It is important to realize that while there was always a strong "native religion" in West Africa, by the early 1400's Islam had become a powerful religious as well as political and economic force. By 1492 the great Negro kingdom of Songhay had already conquered most of West Africa. Songhay accepted the religion of Islam reluctantly at first but later, through her conquests, helped to spread it over much of West Africa.

Songhay was one of the last of the great empires of West Africa. One of the first was Ghana, already an ancient civilization at the time of the Norman invasion of England in 1066. A history of Ghana written by the Muslim scholar Al-Bakri in 1067 presents a detailed picture of the wealth, the pomp and circumstance at the court of the reigning African king, Teraminen. As head of the state religion Teraminen was not himself a Muslim, but he permitted the Muslim traders from the north to establish a small Muslim town convenient to the capital. Under his rule, Ghana pacified all of the surrounding territory, thereby ensuring the safety of the trade routes to North Africa and to the Nile Valley.

Al-Bakri wrote that the king of Ghana "is the master of a

large empire and of a formidable power." He could "put two hundred thousand warriors into the field," including some forty thousand archers. "When the king gives audience to his people," Al-Bakri wrote, ". . . he sits in a pavilion around which stand ten pages holding shields and gold-mounted swords. On his right hand are the sons of the princes of the empire, splendidly clad with gold plaited in their hair. The governor of the city is seated on the ground in front of the king, and all around him are his counselors in the same position. The gate of the chamber is guarded by dogs of an excellent breed. . . . they wear collars of gold and silver, ornamented with metals."

Five hundred years later, another writer named Mahmud Kati, in a book called the *Tarikh al-Fattash,* or "The Chronicle of the Seeker," writes of another King of Ghana, Kanissa' ai, who reigned in the seventh century, and who owned one thousand blooded horses, each of which had three personal attendants and "slept only on a carpet with a silken rope for a halter." Such legends, while probably magnified by time and distance, do offer some perspective on the grandeur and magnificence of a brilliant African kingdom which flourished for more than a thousand years.

Successor to Ghana, and even greater in wealth, power, and extent, was the empire of Mali which developed from the little state of Kangaba, once a vassal state of Ghana. Mansa Musa ascended the throne in 1312 and during the next twenty-five years made Mali into one of the largest empires of the world. He brought the Western Sudan under a unified system of law, gave dependable protection to the trade routes, and expanded his rule over such cities as Timbuktu (an important center of learning) and Walata on the southern Sahara. Later, Mansa Musa embraced Islam, and in 1324 made a historic pilgrimage to Mecca. It is said that he took with him and gave away so much gold as to upset the market in Cairo through which he passed. He is described by Al-Omri, a contemporary scholar living in Cairo during the period, as "the most powerful, the richest, the most fortunate, and the most feared by his enemies. . . ." Ambassadors from Mali represented their government in Morocco, Cairo and other centers of power. Scholars from the University of Timbuktu were received at the great universities in Egypt and Spain. And Mansa Musa brought back with him from Egypt scholars, architects, and men of science to enhance his court and to further facilitate his empire building in West Africa.

The Empire of Songhay flourished in West Africa until modern times, although its founding dates back to the ancient city of Gao on the Niger River almost a thousand years ago. Under the rule of Dia Kossoi, Songhay began a slow period of growth, and after three hundred years Gao was wealthy enough to attract the eye of Mansa Musa, the great king of Mali, who sent his generals to subdue it. But Mali was already over-extended, and Gao regained her independence in 1375. The king who established Songhay as a great empire was Sunni Ali who ruled from 1464 to 1492, the year Columbus discovered America. From 1493 to 1529 the empire was ruled by Askia Muhammed, or "Askia the Great," under whose rule the boundaries of Songhay were extended even further so that she eventually came to rival the empire of Mali in size and importance.

While Songhay subdued most of the neighboring peoples, the Hausa and Mossi tribes were able to repell the incursions of her mighty armies. These fabled warriors held out against repeated invasions by other Moslem groups too, and later stopped, temporarily, even the European conquerors with their modern sophisticated weapons. The Hausa and the Mossi were finally overrun by the Fulani, a Negro Moslem tribal group which struck from the Sahara in the nineteenth century. The Fulani were in turn eventually defeated in 1861 by the British, who thereafter established the colony of Nigeria, which is one of the foremost states of modern West Africa.

As we have already noted, the economy, art forms, political systems and religions of the West African people ranged widely. However, these unique traditions could not withstand the corroding effect of European colonial expansion, especially as Africa became a prime source for slave labor needed to fill the demands of settlement in the New World.

Just as there are misconceptions about the cultural background of the slaves brought to America from West Africa, so there are misconceptions about the way slaves were acquired to supply the markets in the New World. The general pattern was as follows: Europeans usually made contacts with the highly organized political kingdoms on the west coast of Africa, and it was these kingdoms which supplied them with slaves. These coastal empires had long engaged in periodic wars with the inland peoples who were generally weaker in political and military organization. Prisoners were usually taken on a small scale but, before European contact, there is no evidence that the sale of slaves was an established practice.

Only when Europeans began to purchase slaves for commercial purposes did "slave wars" become common. What had once been a system of limited political warfare now quickly became an organized system of raids into the interior to capture entire native populations who would then be sold on the coast to European traders. The traders supplied the slave raiders with guns and ammunition and encouraged ever larger raids to meet the needs of the burgeoning slave markets in the Americas.

Probably not until much later, sometime in the late 1700's, were slaves actually taken in large numbers from the more highly developed nations of West Africa; and then only as a result of the defeat of one major kingdom by another. There is a traditional belief that West African slaves were much desired for their highly-skilled labor potential. While it is undoubtedly true that many artisans and other skilled craftsmen were taken from the developed civilizations of West Africa, most of the captured blacks came from the more remote interior villages because European slave traders were not particularly interested in whether the slaves were skilled or not.

By accident or plan, Portuguese and Spanish slavers helped preserve a considerable amount of African culture in their American colonies. Their general practice of keeping slave families intact was invaluable in this regard. The Catholic Church played an important role in the Portuguese and Spanish treatment of slaves, especially in South America and other places where Catholicism was the dominant religion; in ordering that religious instruction be offered the slaves, the Church helped reduce illiteracy and increased the ease with which the slaves adapted to their new and hostile environment. Then, too, few Spanish and Portuguese women emigrated to the New World, and the Church encouraged marriages between Iberian colonists and both Negro and Indian women. By 1630, Africans had established a successful state, the Republic of Palmares, in northeastern Brazil. The town of Palmares, sixty miles southwest of the Brazilian coastal city of Recife, is still in existence.

Although the African family was virtually destroyed by the peculiar form that slavery took in North America, some vestigial remnants of African culture have survived here. For example, many Negro mothers retained a West African tradition in the naming of children. Many slave children, especially those born along the Georgia and South Carolina coasts, were

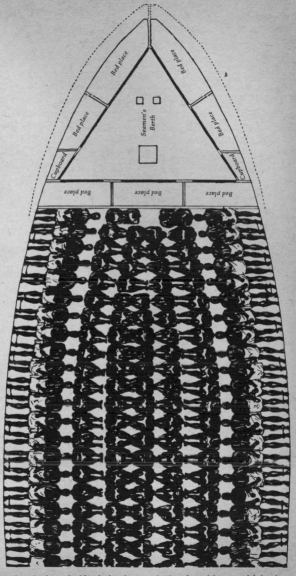

Overhead view, half of the lower deck of a ship to which slaves were manacled for the long voyage from Africa to the colonies. *(Schomburg Collection, New York Public Library)*

Sectional view of the slave ship, from water line upward.
(Schomburg Collection, New York Public Library)

named for the time of their birth, *i.e.*, a month, a day, or even
a time of day. In some areas slaves retained certain elements
of their African religions and incorporated them later into
Christian rituals and practice. In general, however, the North
American slave was so violently and so completely severed
from his past that American Negroes have retained few cultural links with their ancestral homeland.

One of the great tragedies of the slave system in America
was its effect on slave families. Marriage among slaves was
not recognized by law and stable relationships were discour-
aged because they tended to interfere with the ready availability of the slave for sale or procreation. Sometimes "com-
mon-law" marriages were permitted, although separation of
wives and husbands was not subject to any "rights" inherent
in such relationships. It developed inevitably that, in the absence of a stable marriage relationship respected by the slaveholders, the slave family in North America came to be dominated by the mother into whose sole care the children were
committed. Among South American and West Indian Negroes, where the rupture of the family through sale of one of
the parents was less frequent, a patriarchal pattern of family
relationships was the rule.

The first Negroes to arrive in the Western Hemisphere were *not* the "twenty Negars" traded in Jamestown harbor by a Dutch captain in 1619. A Negro, Pedro Alonzo Niño, was the navigator of the Niña, one of the ships Christopher Columbus sailed to the New World in 1492. Neflo de Olaña was among thirty Negroes serving with Balboa when the Spanish explorer discovered the Pacific Ocean. Cortez led a company of Negro explorers into Mexico, where they planted and harvested the New World's first wheat crop. And Estevan, a Negro scout for the explorer Narváez, was the first non-Indian to penetrate what is now Arizona. Hundreds of Negroes served as explorers in the Jesuit-led French parties that entered Canada, as well as in later expeditions that probed the upper regions of the Mississippi River. One, Jean Baptiste Point du Sable, was the founder of Chicago.

With such a noble and heroic beginning, how did the Negro

become a slave in America? In anticipating this question, let us examine some historical aspects of slavery.

World Slavery

Initially, slaves were not identified with any particular race or group of people. The earliest known slaves became slaves by virtue of being prisoners of war. As with all enduring social customs, slavery underwent changes in style. At first, prisoner-slaves were held as the property of a victorious state. Later, with the organization of slave markets, individual ownership of slaves became one of the first "status symbols."

In Europe, the fourth and fifth centuries A.D. saw serfdom replace the former practice of chattel slavery. The serf was a peasant "bound to the land" of his lord and working without pay. By being attached permanently to one family, the serf enjoyed an advantage over the chattel slave: the serf was able to keep his own family intact.

During the Middle Ages religious differences formed the rationale for slavery. Christians were enslaved by Moslems. Later, Christians themselves enslaved Moslems and other non-Christians.

The American Experience

The first English settlement in America was established at Jamestown, Virginia in 1607. The English colonies were desperate for labor needed to push inland to clear the forests and cultivate the land. There was a short-lived attempt to use Indians as laborers, and hundreds were enslaved. However, the Indians proved unadaptable to large-scale farming operations and many died in the fields. The search for labor then focused upon white Englishmen who were brought to the colonies as indentured servants or "bondsmen."

Most bondsmen were extremely poor, many having been taken from European debtors' prisons. Others were convicted felons. Many poor Englishmen were so eager to escape the repressive class structure of their home islands that they signed contracts as bondsmen in return for passage to America. Bondsmen usually served for seven years, although some were bound for twice that time. Bondsmen were not chattels in the same sense as were slaves. It should be noted, however, that bondsmen could be (and often were) traded and sold to new holders. They were permitted to be litigants in the colonial courts, and a few bondsmen sued their holders for illegal detention. This was especially true of those who were sold to new holders who attempted, by various devices, to lengthen their period of bound service. But the majority of bondsmen fulfilled their contracts and, in accordance with existing laws and practices, were then released. When the supply of voluntary indentured servants began to dwindle, it became a widespread practice to kidnap English men, women, and children to be sold into bondage in the New World. By the middle of the seventeenth century approximately 12,000 white bondsmen were serving in Virginia alone.

The importation of Negro bondsmen dates from 1619, when twenty Negroes were purchased by English colonists from a Dutch warship docked at Jamestown, Virginia. It must be emphasized that those twenty human beings came ashore as bondsmen, *not* as slaves, and Virginia court records support this fact. In 1624, John Phillip, one of the twenty Negroes, was a witness in a lawsuit. Under then existing English law, a *slave* had no legal status; he could not sue, be sued, or give testimony. Other records show that the child of one couple among the twenty Negroes was later baptized a Christian. English law provided that persons who had been baptized became enfranchised. Conversion to Christianity was the first step many slaves took toward what they hoped would be eventual freedman status.

As the colonies grew and prospered, it became increasingly clear that the supply of bondsmen would be inadequate. To encourage white emigration to America, the English government enacted a series of new laws to improve working conditions and to make it easier for bondsmen to become landowners after their service ended. Substantial numbers of both white and black bondsmen abandoned agriculture and became industrial workers. Other bondsmen were impatient for freedom and ran away from their masters. It was relatively easy for a white bondsman to move into another community where he could become a trapper or fur trader, but it was impossible for the Negro bondsman to blend into the populace of a strange neighborhood because of his darker skin.

This raises a psychological point that remains valid today: Because the Negro was "different" in appearance, many whites justified their different treatment of him. That the vast majority of Negroes were non-Christians in a proclaimed Christian land added another rationalization for slavery.

Francisko, claimed to be the first settler of Brooklyn, New York.
(Schomburg Collection, New York Public Library)

Fifty-one years after the Jamestown venture, Virginia law reflected the abandonment of attempts to bring white bondsmen to America. A new law provided that all bondsmen coming to Virginia by sea "shall be slaves for their lives," and that those who came by land were to serve a period of apprenticeship. In 1667, another Virginia law had repealed the earlier statute enfranchising Negroes who converted to Christianity. Finally, in 1682, Virginia law reduced all non-Christians, including later converts, to permanent slave status.

In 1708, Virginia held about 12,000 Negro slaves, while approximately 1,000 were being imported each year. By 1782, the Negro slave population of the state had reached 260,000. During the years between 1715 and 1750, slave importations for all the colonies increased from an average of 2,500 to an average of 7,500 a year.

For the more enlightened colonial leaders, the fight against slavery was part of the fight for basic freedom. Throughout the entire Revolutionary era Benjamin Franklin raised a powerful voice against slavery. In 1774, Thomas Jefferson included in his *Summary View of the Rights of British America*, a statement that all the colonies wanted slavery abolished. Jefferson also accused England of subverting colonial attempts to end the slave trade. That same year, largely through the efforts of Franklin and Jefferson, the Continental Congress agreed to bar the importation of slaves after December 1, 1775.

While the Continental Congress was drafting the Declaration of Independence, Jefferson submitted to that body what John Adams called a "vehement" denunciation of slavery, but Jefferson failed to convince Congress to make abolition a part of the historic 1776 document.

Although the Negro did not have the same rights as the white colonialists, the Revolutionary period produced several distinguished Negroes who contributed to America's cultural growth. Jupiter Hammon, a slave on Long Island, wrote poetry widely read throughout the colonies. Hammon tried to purchase his freedom but was unable to raise enough money. When he failed to gain his own liberty, he finally accepted slavery as his personal misfortune, but continued to urge manumission of young Negroes.

Gustavus Vassa was kidnapped by slavers when he was eleven years old. Brought to America, Vassa became the slave of a Philadelphia merchant who later freed him. Vassa moved to England and wrote an autobiography that to this day remains one of the most detailed accounts of the life of an eighteenth-century slave.

Phillis Wheatley, born in Africa around 1753, was enslaved and taken to Boston, Massachusetts. Her masters recognized the girl's intelligence and young Phillis was taught to read and write. Her first book, *Poems on Various Subjects, Religious and Moral*, was published shortly after her manumission in 1773. She died nine years later, but her fame continued, and she remains one of New England's best-known poets.

There were many other prominent Negroes during the Revolutionary era: John Derham, the first Negro physician in America; Onesimus, a slave who encouraged smallpox inoculations in America because he recalled how successful such

Crispus Attucks, ex-slave, was the first to fall in the Revolutionary War, when he led a group of Boston patriots.
(Schomburg Collection, New York Public Library)

treatment had been in Africa; Paul Cuffe, a Negro who amassed a fortune as a Massachusetts merchant and ship-owner; and Lucy Terry, a slave whose first poetry was published about seven years before Phillis Wheatley was born.

Probably the most accomplished Negro of the Revolutionary period was Benjamin Banneker, a free-born Negro. Born in 1731, Banneker was a scientist and mathematician of such ability that he was one of the first Americans to predict a solar eclipse accurately. Later, he published a series of almanacs that gained him the recognition and support of Jefferson, among other prominent whites. On Jefferson's recommendation the Maryland-born Negro was appointed by President Washington to the commission that surveyed and laid out what is now the District of Columbia.

The tension between England and the colonies erupted in

James Lafayette, a deeply commit-
ted Negro spy and soldier, served
in the Revolutionary army under
Lafayette.
*(Schomburg Collection, New York
Public Library)*

Peter Salem, a former slave, won
fame for shooting down British
Major Pitcairn in the Battle of
Bunker Hill.
*(Schomburg Collection, New York
Public Library)*

violence in Boston, Massachusetts on March 5, 1770. A detachment of British soldiers fired into a group of civilians gathered on historic State Street. Crispus Attucks, a Negro sailor who sought to rally the confused Americans in the face of the British fire, was the first to give his life for America. Later, however, when General George Washington assumed command of the Continental Army in July, 1775, he issued an order excluding all Negroes from service in the war. The British countered by offering freedom to all slaves who joined the Crown's forces. The British move forced Washington to modify his position and permitted free Negroes to serve. But all slaves remained barred from fighting for America's freedom; or their own.

The Battle of Bunker Hill produced two Negro heroes in the colonial struggle for liberty. It was a Negro, Peter Salem, who shot Major Pitcairn, the British commander during that bloody engagement. Salem shot him just as he was telling his troops, "The day is ours!" Another heroic Negro, Salem Poor, was awarded a formal commendation by the Massachusetts legislature for "behaving like an experienced officer as well as . . . a brave and gallant soldier."

By the end of the Revolutionary War, an estimated 5,000 Negro soldiers had served in the Continental Army. In most military groups, white and Negro troops served side by side; in addition, several all-Negro combat units fought in the war, and one such unit was commanded by a Negro officer.

A few free Negroes attained substantial financial success before and following the Revolutionary War. Many bought farms, and there was one recorded case of a free Negro who owned thirty Negro slaves. Generally, however, the free Negroes purchased small and usually exhausted plots of land that yielded neither quality nor quantity.

Although they had escaped from an oppressive relationship with England themselves, the majority of delegates to the Constitutional Convention of 1787 were openly pro-slavery. As if to prove that fact to their heirs, the Founding Fathers provided in the Constitution for a twenty-year extension of the slave trade—the only blot on that otherwise honorable document.

Nevertheless, largely through the efforts of the Quakers and Methodists, the manumission of slaves increased during the Revolutionary period. The first manumission statute was enacted by Maryland in 1752, although the motives for the law were not altogether humanitarian. Maryland was determined to control the actions of irresponsible slaveholders who abandoned their slaves for the community to support when they were old and no longer able to work. The first years of the Republic saw the free Negro population grow very rapidly. Near the end of the eighteenth century nearly three times as many Negroes were free as were slaves.

Another factor accounts for the increase in the free Negro population. Many Negroes were born to free Negro mothers and fathers. However, it is impossible to gauge accurately how many children were born of racially mixed parentage—the children of white women servants and slaves, or of slave mothers and white fathers. As early as 1662 the Virginia legislature had enacted the following law:

> Whereas some doubts have arisen whether children got by any Englishman upon a Negro woman shall be slave or free . . . all children born in this colony shall be bond or free only according to the condition of the mother.

Later, Virginia enacted another law which provided that if a white woman servant married a Negro, she would serve an additional five years. In 1664, Maryland law provided that if a "freeborn white woman" married a slave, she became the servant of her husband's master so long as the husband lived. The law also provided that the children of such a couple became slaves at birth. This law, which made virtual slaves of certain white women, was later repealed to prevent the forced marriage of white women servants to Negroes by unscrupulous masters. Eventually, the white wives of Negroes and their children were elevated to freed status and the large mulatto population among free Negroes was dramatic evidence of the massive miscegenation between whites and Negroes. By 1850, thirty-seven per cent of free Negroes in the United States were classified mulattoes; many were the children of slave mothers whose white masters had "freed" their own offspring.

The Cotton Gin

In 1792, Eli Whitney invented the cotton gin, an event which changed the base of the Southern economy. Cotton quickly became the major Southern crop. In order to grow enough cotton to meet the demand and to keep the cotton gins running, large numbers of workers were needed. This increased demand for labor perpetrated the South's reliance on a slave-labor economy. Once this change was set in motion there was

Typical poster advertising sales of Negroes.
(Schomburg Collection, New York Public Library)

Eli Whitney's cotton gin spurred the growth of the cotton industry and tightened the chains of slavery.
(Schomburg Collection, New York Public Library)

J. M. WILSON

HAVING REMOVED TO THE

CORNER OF ESPLANADE & MOREAU STS.

NEW ORLEANS,

Will keep on hand and be constantly receiving during the season,

LARGE SUPPLIES OF

MARYLAND

AND

VIRGINA NEGROES;

CONSISTING OF

Field Hands, House Servants, Cooks, Seamstresses, Washers and Ironers, Mechanics, &c,

ALL OF WHICH WILL BE SOLD

LOW FOR CASH,

OR, ON TIME, FOR GOOD CITY ACCEPTANCE.

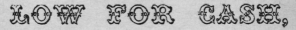

PLANTERS AND PURCHASERS

Generally are respectfully invited to

Call and Examine before Purchasing elsewhere.

From *Harper's Weekly*, 1861—sketch of a slave auction in the South.
(Schomburg Collection, New York Public Library)

little hope that the South would give up its slave holdings. On the contrary, it now had even more reason to hold on to what it had and to try to extend the practice.

While it is undoubtedly true that the growth of "King Cotton" resulted in the expansion of slavery, even before 1792 slavery was a dominant social and economic way of life which the Southerner was not anxious to change. So, as the cotton industry grew, the possibility of a peaceful solution to the slavery question was proportionately lessened.

Now that slavery had an even larger economic base, the slave found himself caught ever more hopelessly in the toils of oppression, with his circumstances increasingly difficult. More time and effort was spent in preventing him from escaping, or in catching him if he did escape. Prices for healthy

Slaves were treated like cattle—
as if they were insensitive to cold,
pain, fear or loneliness.
*(Schomburg Collection, New York
Public Library)*

slaves were higher than they had ever been and the owners worked their slaves harder to realize full returns on their investments. Since slavery had become big business, the possibility of political action to put an end to it became more remote. The full force of the South's political and economic power, reinforced by the efforts of those industrialists in the North and in England who had large sums of money invested in the Southern cotton industry, determinedly frustrated any abolitionist move.

The stage was being set for a major confrontation. Except for an occasional manumission (and the laws of manumission became increasingly severe), the typical slave could look forward only, save for the unlikely prospects of successful revolt or escape, to giving the whole of his life to obedient service to his master.

Slave Revolts

One of the persistent American myths concerning the Negro slave is that he did nothing to protest his enslavement. This

To prevent their escape, slaves were shackled, tethered, or, like this woman, hindered by such devices as iron horns and bells.
(*Schomburg Collection, New York Public Library*)

myth is patently and demonstrably at variance with the facts. Although no single slave revolt succeeded, slave communities never lacked the contagion of revolt. Indeed, American history is marked by a series of slave revolts. Between 1663 and 1864, at least a hundred and nine separate slave revolts occurred on land, while between 1699 and 1845, fifty-five revolts took place on slave ships at sea.

New York City was the scene of a massive slave uprising in the spring of 1712. Several whites were shot and buildings set afire before the militia quelled the insurrection. Twenty-one Negroes were executed for that revolt. Another slave rebellion occurred in Manhattan in 1741; thirty-one Negroes and five whites (two of them women) were executed for participating in that uprising.

In the South, many slave revolts took place even during the colonial period. Several slaves were burned to death after an unsuccessful revolt in 1720 near Charleston, South Carolina. Ten years later, another serious uprising in South Carolina was crushed. Again, in 1739, South Carolina was the scene of three massive revolts among slaves.

Three nineteenth-century slave revolts deserve special mention. On September 1, 1800, eleven hundred slaves set out to destroy Richmond, Virginia. The force, led by Gabriel Prosser and Jack Bowler, planned a three-pronged attack on the town. While rain-swollen streams delayed the attack, two Negro slaves revealed the plot. Prosser was captured two months later. He, Bowler, and thirty-three other Negroes were executed.

In 1800, Denmark Vesey, of Charleston, South Carolina, bought his freedom for six hundred dollars. Later, he worked as a carpenter in the area and used his spare time to study the French Revolution and the successful slave revolts in Haiti. In 1822, after twenty-two years of planning and study, Vesey organized a slave plot aimed at the seizure of Charleston. But Vesey, like Prosser, was betrayed by a slave who informed his master. Authorities arrested a hundred and thirty-nine Negroes and executed forty-seven, including Vesey; thirty-seven other Negroes were banished from the United States, and four white men who had encouraged Vesey were fined and imprisoned.

The third major slave revolt of the nineteenth century was led by Nat Turner. Turner was a mystic and his actions were based on a vision that he had been selected by God to lead the slaves against their white oppressors. What became known as

the Southampton County Insurrection was, if not the largest, the most violent slave revolt in the history of this country.
Turner masterminded the rebellion, but his strategy was directed by his visions and the heavenly voices he heard rather
than by logic and reason. Leading a small band of slaves, he
descended on Southampton County, Virginia, on the night
of August 21, 1831. The first victims were his master and the
four members of his household. Taking arms and recruiting
slaves as they went, the small group soon grew into a well-
armed band of about seventy men. They marched toward the
county seat, killing white slaveholders and their families as
they encountered them. In all, Turner's band killed ten men,
fourteen women, and thirty-five children. When the revolt was
finally broken on August 22, 1831, Turner went into hiding
for two months. During this time, the entire South was in turmoil, fearing a full-scale revolution. Not until his capture and
execution on November 11, did the situation quieten. It took
three thousand troops and two months to track down this

Heeding an inner call to lead "the children of Egypt" out of
bondage, Nat Turner led a revolt that threw the South into
turmoil.
(Schomburg Collection, New York Public Library)

Mary, an escaped slave, chose to jump from a window in Washington, D.C., rather than face being returned to the South.
(Schomburg Collection, New York Public Library)

"prophet" of freedom and, even after his death, the nation remained troubled. Nat Turner's Revolt demonstrated to the whites of America, both North and South, that many Negroes were willing to kill and to die to achieve freedom. The nation was to debate this issue for many years and to face the same problem again with John Brown's Raid. But not until the Civil War was this issue to be met head-on.

Revolts were not the only means Negroes used to rebel against captivity. Every conceivable form of resistance was employed, including work slowdowns, infanticide, sabotage, suicide, and escape.

Some writers of the early nineteenth century refer to the impossibility of forcing the Negro slaves to work to capacity, except when working for themselves. In the fields, they had to be watched constantly and supervised by the plantation

overseer. Yet, when Negroes cultivated their own land or were working toward buying their own or a relative's freedom, their efficiency often surprised slaveholders. Malingering, or feigning sickness, was a favorite device used by the slave to avoid working the white man's fields. Petty sabotage in the form of breaking and misusing tools or laming animals, and more serious acts such as arson and poisoning, were further evidence of the Negro's protest against servitude.

Infanticide and suicide were widely used as a demonstration of rebellion. Mothers frequently smothered their newborn children rather than see them grow up slaves. And suicide was prevalent enough to be singled out by the plantation owners and clergy as the worst of crimes. Those who destroyed themselves were denied Christian burial or any official observance of their passing.

A runaway slave tries to protect his family from bloodhounds.
(*Schomburg Collection, New York Public Library*)

The westward expansion of the United States demanded a labor force that could, within the context of nineteenth-century American economic morality, be provided only by slave labor. The early 1800's saw a one-thousand-mile area, stretching from South Carolina to Texas, become one of the world's most productive agricultural regions. The area was especially suited to long growing periods, thus permitting several crops to be harvested in a single season. The key crop was cotton and that plant became virtual king of the Southern United States.

The Louisiana Purchase of 1803 opened up additional lands for cultivation and provided the foundation for what came to

Oshkosh, Wisconsin, is named for this Negro-Indian Chief.
(Schomburg Collection, New York Public Library)

be known as America's "Manifest Destiny." That doctrine was viewed differently in the North and the South. Southerners, by and large, viewed "Manifest Destiny" as the simple policy of expansion across the continent by whatever means were available. For many Northerners, westward expansion and "Manifest Destiny" meant establishing an "Empire for liberty."

While spectacular economic events were taking place in the slave-holding South, the anti-slavery movement was gaining strength in the North. The Negro had not become an important social or economic factor in the North, mainly because slavery had never been firmly entrenched there. Hence, anti-slavery sentiment in the North was more pronounced than in the South. However, sentiment had not crystallized in terms of exactly what should be done about slavery, or how. Many Northerners were indifferent to the entire question. On the other hand, a large segment of the population was against slavery in principle and looked forward to its eventual end. Such "moderates" of the pre-Civil War period hoped to "contain" slavery in the states where it existed, expecting its ultimate demise as a socio-economic anachronism unable to survive its own weight. The radical abolitionist movement advocated absolute and immediate freedom for the Negro. But it was opposed by many Northerners who feared the sudden release of four million Negroes into an established white society as a major threat to social stability.

Probably the most vocal of all the white abolitionists was William Lloyd Garrison, the fiery editor of *The Liberator*. Garrison's inflammatory anti-slavery editorials represented the height of nineteenth-century American militancy, and in 1835, that militancy almost cost him his life when a group of well-dressed Bostonians attacked and beat him. The incident moved another Bostonian, Wendell Phillips, to abandon his own career and become Garrison's principal aide. Phillips, a lawyer and Harvard graduate, rose to prominence in the abolition movement after his 1837 speech in Boston protesting the murder of Elijah P. Lovejoy, an Alton, Illinois, abolitionist editor. Phillips' trained legal mind was a necessary balance for Garrison's emotionalism.

The abolitionist campaign was the channel through which the American Negro press came into being. John B. Russwurm, an alumnus of Bowdoin College, was the first Negro to graduate with a degree from an American college. In 1827, he founded the nation's first Negro newspaper, *Freedom's*

CAUTION!!

COLORED PEOPLE

OF BOSTON, ONE & ALL,

You are hereby respectfully CAUTIONED and
advised, to avoid conversing with the

Watchmen and Police Officers of Boston,

For since the recent ORDER OF THE MAYOR &
ALDERMEN, they are empowered to act as

KIDNAPPERS

AND

Slave Catchers,

And they have already been actually employed in
KIDNAPPING, CATCHING, AND KEEPING
SLAVES. Therefore, if you value your LIBERTY,
and the *Welfare of the Fugitives* among you, *Shun*
them in every possible manner, as so many *HOUNDS*
on the track of the most unfortunate of your race.

Keep a Sharp Look Out for KIDNAPPERS, and have TOP EYE open.

APRIL 24, 1851.

The Boston Vigilance Committee aided the abolitionists in many
ways. This placard warned Negroes to beware of kidnappers.
(Schomburg Collection, New York Public Library)

Journal, in New York City. Ten years later, with Phillip A. Bell as publisher and Samuel E. Cornish as editor, *The Weekly Advocate* was launched. Frederick Douglass later began publishing *The North Star.* Two prominent Negro historians also contributed to world awareness of the evils of slavery: William C. Nell, a Bostonian, devoted his life to writing a series of scholarly historical works, while William Wells Brown abandoned a career as a physician to become a historian.

Several Southern states responded to abolitionist pressure by enacting or strengthening manumission laws, and Maryland adopted a policy aimed at colonizing the slaves in Africa. With some financial aid from the federal government, the American Colonization Society was formed in 1817, virtually °creating what is now the African state of Liberia. More than a thousand manumitted slaves were sent to that infant nation, many solely on the condition that upon release they would leave American soil and "return" to Africa.

The general condition of the manumission laws provided that freed slaves leave the states where they had lived; that requirement sent large numbers of Negroes flooding into the North. The influx contributed to a stiffening of attitudes against Negroes in several communities. For example, between 1807 and 1838, New York, Pennsylvania, New Jersey, and Connecticut either disenfranchised Negroes or required extremely high property holdings as a qualification to vote. In Ohio, each freed Negro entering the state was required to post a bond of five hundred dollars. Indiana and Illinois took similar restrictive measures. Generally, the South viewed the freed Negro as an infection that could destroy the entire framework of slavery. The North was afraid that the free Negro would affect the labor market adversely and resented the fact that Negroes generally without property holdings, were a potential drain upon taxpaying landowners.

Actually, in several American cities, free Negroes were a significant segment of the taxpaying population. By 1832, free Negroes in Philadelphia had amassed taxable property worth 350,000 dollars, a figure that rose to more than 400,000 dollars by 1847. In Cincinnati, Ohio, Negro property holdings totalled 228,000 dollars by 1840. Negro economic progress

---

In 1845, Frederick Douglass, foremost Negro abolitionist, wrote a narrative that described his unusual career and told of his slave origins.
(Schomburg Collection, New York Public Library)

was not restricted to the North. Jehu Jones, a free Negro,
owned the largest hotel interest in Charleston, South Carolina,
with holdings estimated in excess of 40,000 dollars. In New
Orleans, Thomas Lafon, a merchant, had an estimated fortune of 500,000 dollars; while in Macon, Georgia, Solomon
Humphries was that area's most prosperous grocer with assets
exceeding 20,000 dollars. The 1830 federal census also reported that some 3,777 Negro heads of families were slaveowners, with holdings concentrated in North and South Carolina, Virginia, and Maryland.

The Underground Railroad

Although the slave trade was officially outlawed in 1808, the
only immediate practical change was that it became an unofficial part of American life. The development of internal slave
trading and slave breeding became major Southern enterprises
as the nation expanded westward. Slave breeding for the auction block was unquestionably the most dehumanizing aspect
of slavery. The auction block was often the spur that sent the
Negro on a break for freedom. Runaway slaves became, in
fact, such a major problem to the South that in 1793 a benign
Federal government enacted the first of two fugitive slave
laws. The laws required "all good citizens" to assist Federal
marshals and their deputies in apprehending runaway slaves.

Fugitive slave laws were heavily weighted against the Negro. He was denied a jury trial in Federal courts; his testimony was inadmissible; and the unsupported sworn statement
of an alleged but absent owner often was the main evidence
offered against a Negro accused of being a runaway slave. In
reaction, many Northerners formerly unconcerned about slavery soon became ardent abolitionists. Some Northern states
even passed local laws nullifying the fugitive statutes.

With the return of the veterans from the War of 1812,
many Negroes first heard of Canada and realized that freedom lay just across the Ohio River. Soon it became com-
monly known among the slaves that by following "the North
Star" they could escape into free territory. Slaveowners were
so mystified by the increase in runaways that they began to
speculate that their slaves had escaped on some sort of "underground railroad."

The Railroad, or "U.G." was, in fact, an elaborate network
of secret contacts between free Negroes and white sympathiz-

Underground Railroad "brakeman" William Still kept a record documenting the hardships and struggles of the fleeing slaves. See pages 40–41.
(Schomburg Collection, New York Public Library)

The Vigilance Committee resurrected Henry Brown who was shipped in a box from Richmond, Virginia, to Philadelphia, Pennsylvania.
(Schomburg Collection, New York Public Library)

W Still

THE

UNDERGROUND RAIL ROAD.

A RECORD

OF

FACTS, AUTHENTIC NARRATIVES, LETTERS, &c.,

Narrating the Hardships Hair-breadth Escapes and Death Struggles

OF THE

Slaves in their efforts for Freedom,

AS RELATED

BY THEMSELVES AND OTHERS, OR WITNESSED BY THE AUTHOR;

TOGETHER WITH

SKETCHES OF SOME OF THE LARGEST STOCKHOLDERS, AND

MOST LIBERAL AIDERS AND ADVISERS,

OF THE ROAD.

BY

WILLIAM STILL,

For many years connected with the Anti-Slavery Office in Philadelphia, and Chairman
of the Acting Vigilant Committee of the Philadelphia Branch of
the Underground Rail Road.

Illustrated with 70 fine Engravings by Bensell. Schell and others. and
Portraits from Photographs from Life.

Thou shalt not deliver unto his master the servant that has escaped from his master unto thee.—*Deut.* xxiii. 15.

SOLD ONLY BY SUBSCRIPTION.

PHILADELPHIA:
PORTER & COATES,
822, CHESTNUT STREET.
1872.

ers, set up to help escaped slaves reach freedom. There is no accurate count of the number of Negroes who actually passed through the system, although one widely accepted estimate is that each year during the thirty years following 1830, as many as two thousand slaves traveled the U.G. to freedom. Supported by Quakers and other friendly whites, the U.G. depended mainly upon Negro bravery for much of its success. Among the many Negroes whose names were prominent in the movement were those of William Wells Brown, George DeBaptist, Martin Dalany, Frederick Douglass, James Forten, Henry Highland Garnett, J. W. Loguen, Lewis Hayden, Charles Remond, David Ruggles, William Still, Sojourner Truth, David Walker, Samuel Ward, and Theodore S. Wright.

One of the bravest and most dramatic operators of the U.G. was a Negro woman, Harriet Tubman. After escaping from slavery at the age of twenty-nine, Miss Tubman made repeated trips back into the South to bring out other Negroes. She is credited personally with leading more than three hundred slaves North to freedom. Miss Tubman was apparently a peculiarly single-minded young woman who often brandished a loaded revolver to urge on frightened or timid members of her caravans. At one time, slaveholders offered as much as 40,000 dollars for her capture, but she survived and served with Union Army forces during the Civil War, first as a nurse and later as a spy behind Confederate lines.

Issues: North and South

Because of the emotions it aroused, slavery became a symbol of the growing chasm between Northern and Southern economic interests and cultural outlooks. Visible manifestation of the difference was that one region continued to hold slaves; the other did not. Each sought to influence the newly-developing Western territories. The presence or absence of slaves in those territories (which looked forward to entering the Union as states) came to be interpreted as a practical symbol of the political, social, and economic philosophies of the people who lived in them.

Our young nation was already deeply involved in sectional issues before slavery became the recognized cause of war. Conflicting economic interests were latent but powerful forces in the controversy. The North, with its small farms and free labor, found it difficult to sympathize with Southern planta-

Harriet Tubman, one of the most famous Underground Railroad
conductors, threatened any slave who wanted to turn back.
(Schomburg Collection, New York Public Library)

tions operating on slave labor. Southern planters, in search
of cheap commodities through free trade, were angered by
high tariffs that protected the Northern industrialists but frustrated the South's desire for open markets. Thousands of European immigrants, arriving at the Eastern ports and settling
in the North and Midwest, threatened to upset the political
balance between the North and South.

The abolitionists demanded the end of slavery in the name
of a "higher law" ordained by God, a law to which all state
and Federal laws should conform. It was argued that the
brotherhood of man was explicit in the Scriptures and implicit

Harriet Beecher Stowe

Harriet Beecher Stowe's *Uncle Tom's Cabin* lighted "a million campfires
in front of the embattled hosts of slavery." The first edition sold 5,000
copies in one week and 300,000 during its first year published.
(Schomburg Collection, New York Public Library)

UNCLE TOM'S CABIN;

OR,

LIFE AMONG THE LOWLY.

BY

HARRIET BEECHER STOWE.

VOL. I.

BOSTON:
JOHN P. JEWETT & COMPANY.
CLEVELAND, OHIO:
JEWETT, PROCTOR & WORTHINGTON.
1852.

in the Declaration of Independence, that it was morally and legally unjust to exclude Negroes from the benefits of either.

If any one thing most affected the mood and temper of abolitionist feeling in the North, it was the publication of a novel by Harriet Beecher Stowe. On March 20, 1852, the first edition of *Uncle Tom's Cabin* was published. This book was to shape pre-Civil War America's image of the slave and his master, and it defined the issues all Americans had to face. It revealed the cruelty and horror of slavery and the human and noble qualities of a people held in bondage. Its major point was that the Negro wanted his freedom from a system founded on brutality and evil, and that he would fight and die for that freedom and the freedom of his family and friends. In the years that followed Harriet Beecher Stowe became the most popular representative of the abolitionist movement and today, *Uncle Tom's Cabin* has become, if sentimental with clichés, a classic of American literature.

Slaveholders rejected both Biblical and political arguments and advanced counterarguments. Southerners used the Bible to "prove" justification of slavery by identifying Negroes as descendants of Ham, forever ordained to be "hewers of wood and drawers of water." Further, the argument continued, there was also historical justification for slavery; since it was practiced by the Greeks and Romans, who gave the world two of its most brilliant civilizations, it must be good for America. Besides, slavery had been sanctioned by such philosophers as Aristotle and John Locke and alleged to be "the normal order of nature and of God," a boon to the African savage and to civilized America alike. Leading Southern spokesmen, extolling the benefits of the system, insisted that slavery not only civilized the savage and made him part of a Christian society, but also provided the economic security and necessary leisure for Western civilization to express its inherent cultural genius.

The Declaration of Independence's equalitarian doctrines were interpreted by the South as having no application to slaves because they had had no part in its framing, and were, at the time of its issuance, considered to be a "lower order of beings."

The Slave Codes

In addition to philosophical answers to the abolitionists, the South also issued a concrete answer: the Slave Codes. The

Codes dealt with all facets of slave life, from the barring of private meetings (none were permitted unless a white man was present) to prohibition against entering into or maintaining legal contracts. Violation of the Codes was punishable by penalties ranging from whipping to branding. As the money from cotton became more important, slaveholders generally refrained from administering punishments that would leave a slave permanently crippled. The breaking of Negroes on the wheel was replaced by merciless floggings. Sometimes more stubborn slaves were burned to death at the stake. Escape was the most serious offense against the Slave Codes, and often punishment was meted out on the spot if an escaped slave were captured.

The slave system grew out of plantation life, and any understanding of slave existence requires an examination of the plantation. The plantation was an organized community, the administration of which rested in the hands of either the owner or, in the majority of cases, a head overseer.

The plantation center was the owner's home. Next came the overseer's home, the stables, smokehouses and corncribs, and other storage areas. Nearby were the slave quarters, usually one-room huts with earthen floors. With the cash investment involved, it is strange that so many slaveholders gave their human property such poor care. Often slaves were denied sufficient food and clothing; pregnant Negro women were forced to work in the fields and many were unable to bear healthy children.

The conditions under which the slaves lived were frequently ignored by the Church although some denominations, notably the Unitarians, were consistently anti-slavery. In some sections of the South, the churches actually upheld the practice of slavery. Early in the nineteenth century, the Methodist Church attacked slavery as a moral blight upon America. But by 1836, the Methodists declared they had no "right, wish, or intention of interfering in the civil and political relations between master and slave as it existed in the slaveholding states of the Union." Moreover, many Southern clergymen devoted much of their time to writing pamphlets and lecturing on the alleged inferiority of the Negro. The tension within American religious organizations reached a dramatic point in 1844, when the Baptists divided over sending slaveholding missionaries into the expanding Southwest. Similarly, the Methodists also split over whether one of their ecclesiastical officers,

Bishop James Andrew, could hold such high office and retain the slaves he had acquired through marriage.

The Missouri Compromise

The slavery issue was a constant shadow over the westward expansion of the United States. The portion of the Louisiana Purchase that became the Missouri Territory grew steadily in population and in 1818, the Territory sought admission to the Union as a full-fledged state. Because so many of the Territory's white inhabitants had come from the South, it was assumed that Missouri would join the Union as a slave state. New York Congressman James Tallmadge, a pro-abolitionist, set out to prevent the assumption becoming fact. Tallmadge tried to amend the bill proposing the Territory's admission so that the importation of slaves would be barred by the state's constitution. He also wanted the eventual emancipation of all slaves who had been born in the Territory. The Tallmadge amendment passed the House of Representatives in February, 1819, but the Senate rejected the proposal.

When Alabama joined the Union in 1819, its admission continued a numerical balance in the Senate between the slave and free states. That balance was threatened in 1820, when Maine was proposed for admission and Southern politicians were forced into a compromise. The separate bills sponsoring Maine and Missouri were combined into one single measure. Under the compromise scheme, slavery would not be *prohibited* in the Missouri state constitution. In a sense, the Tallmadge faction suffered a defeat. The liberals, however, were able to promote one important stipulation, as a result of which Congress required a pledge from the Missouri legislature that its new constitution would not abridge the rights of United States citizens, thus protecting those freedmen living in the state.

The Dred Scott Decision

In 1834, Dr. John Emerson, a U. S. Army surgeon, moved from Missouri to Illinois. Dr. Emerson took with him Dred Scott, a Negro slave, who later married and raised a family while living with Dr. Emerson in Wisconsin. Dr. Emerson and Scott returned to Missouri in 1838. After Dr. Emerson

died, Scott sued Mrs. Emerson for his freedom on the grounds
that his residence in the free territories of Illinois and Wisconsin had ended his bondage. Mrs. Emerson and her new husband, a prominent abolitionist Congressman, Dr. C. C. Chaffee, developed a plan. The Chaffees wanted to get the Scott
case into a Federal court and hoped that a favorable decision
for the Negro servant would create a precedent upon which
other slaves could gain freedom with the backing of the ju-
diciary. To avoid having Dr. Chaffee appear in court as a
defendant slaveholder, Scott was technically "sold" to Mrs.
Chaffee's brother, J. F. A. Sanford. The case was heard in

Dred Scott and his wife Harriet. The Dred Scott Decision temporarily
furthered the cause of the anti-slavery ranks.
(*Schomburg Collection, New York Public Library*)

Although John Brown was captured, tried and executed after his raid
on Harper's Ferry, intense feelings were aroused.
(Schomburg Collection, New York Public Library)

several lower courts and, eventually, reached the U. S. Supreme Court. With Southerners dominating the Court, Mr.
Chief Justice Roger Taney handed down a decision that proclaimed slavery a national concept, and freedom a strictly sectional consideration. Justice Taney ruled that Negroes did not
come within the meaning of the Constitution's "people of the

United States." The Court held that a Negro had "no rights which a white man need respect."

In a very real sense, the Civil War began in Kansas, where abolitionists and pro-slavery forces confronted each other over the sights of their rifles. On May 21, 1856, pro-slavery forces raided and sacked Lawrence, Kansas. A few days later, John Brown, a religious visionary and abolitionist, led a group of anti-slavery followers into Lawrence and murdered five pro-slavery men. For two years, bands of abolitionists called Jayhawkers, and other pro-slavery guerrillas, terrorized the Kansas countryside. More than two hundred persons were killed and nearly a quarter million dollars' worth of property destroyed before relative calm was restored to the area. Kansas represented an abolitionist victory, for the state's constitution was amended to forbid slavery.

John Brown continued his energetic battle against slavery and capped his abolitionist career with the raid on Harper's Ferry, Virginia. Brown intended to make Harper's Ferry a stronghold where escaping Negroes could assemble and press their campaign for freedom. On October 16, 1859, Brown and a handful of his guerrillas seized the Federal arsenal and took possession of the town. Federal troops led by Col. Robert E. Lee attacked the town and, after a bloody battle, Brown and a few of his followers were captured. Brown was hanged on December 2, 1859, and reports of his execution indicate that he went to his death acting the great martyr of the abolitionist movement—warning the nation that what had happened at Harper's Ferry was only a prelude to a real war to end slavery. By 1861, his "prophecy" had become reality and the nation was to be made free of slavery by blood.

4 The Civil War and Emancipation

By the middle of the nineteenth century, there were acute sectional differences as to whether new states admitted to the Union would be slaveholding or free. The Compromise of 1850 attempted to improve relations by setting up a balanced set of conditions for the future admission of new states, and by clarifying the slave issue in the District of Columbia. Thereby, California was admitted to the Union as a free state, New Mexico and Utah territories were organized on the principle of popular sovereignty, and the slave trade was ended in Washington, D. C.

Both sides gained and gave concessions. But the 1850 Compromise could not hold together two sections of the country with such disparate interests. Each became more nationalistic in terms of its own attitudes, and each became more certain that the other must make some extensive social and political modifications if the Union were to be maintained.

Sojourner Truth, ex-slave, mystic, ardent abolition-
ist, receives an autographed photograph of President
Lincoln.
(Schomburg Collection, New York Public Library)

The Republican Position

The Presidential campaign of 1860 ended in a Republican
victory, but the Grand Old Party was not united under one
general philosophy. Led by New York's Senator William H.
Seward, the Conservatives were mildly anti-slavery; their
main concern was enacting legislation that would bring more
rapid growth to the industrial North. After winning the election, Lincoln, the Conservative spokesman, paid a political
debt to Seward by appointing him Secretary of State. The

Radical Republicans were a divided lot. The Old Radicals, led by Thaddeus Stevens and Charles Sumner, were abolitionists openly committed to Negro freedom. The New Radicals, although against slavery in "principle," were most deeply concerned with social benefits for the growing numbers of industrial workers.

Lincoln's election was a bitter blow to the South, which apparently misread Republican views and chalked up the results as a victory for the abolitionists. South Carolina led a secession from the Union, and before Lincoln could be inaugurated, Florida, Georgia, Alabama, Mississippi, Louisiana, and Texas had also left the Union.

On the morning of April 12, 1861, Confederate forces opened fire on Fort Sumter in Charleston Harbor. President Lincoln had sought to avoid a military clash, but now he was forced to use troops to preserve the Union. His decision forced Virginia to take sides, and Virginia joined the Confederacy. Arkansas, North Carolina, and Tennessee also joined the Confederate States of America; four slave states (Delaware, Missouri, Kentucky, and Maryland) remained in the Union. The western counties of Virginia broke with the South, formed the state of West Virginia, and joined the Union.

With the nation split, Lincoln made it plain that his greatest aim was to reunite and preserve the Union. Although the President personally opposed slavery on humanitarian grounds, it was his conviction that the Federal government had no right to prohibit slavery in the South. Lincoln did, however, believe Congress should prevent slavery from being extended into the Western territories. His opposition to the Westward growth of slavery was based upon the fear that slave labor would have an adverse effect upon the growth of the newly opened sections of the nation. In a letter he wrote to Horace Greeley shortly after the war began, the President stated his position:

Abraham Lincoln, sixteenth President of the United States.
(Schomburg Collection, New York Public Library)

My paramount object in this struggle is to save the Union and is not either to save or destroy slavery. If I could save the Union without freeing any slave, I would do it; if I could save it by freeing all the slaves, I would do it; and if I could save it by freeing some and leaving others alone, I would also do it. What I do about slavery and the colored race, I do because I believe it helps to save the Union.

As soon as Union forces penetrated the South, it became clear that some more definitive solution was required concerning the Negro. Runaway slaves often met Union forces and attached themselves to the blue-clad troops. On the plantations overrun by Union soldiers the Negroes were nominally slaves, but technically free. Many field commanders found themselves not only waging war against rebels, but also forced to provide food and shelter for large numbers of homeless slaves.

A small scandal erupted in July, 1861, when it was learned that President Lincoln had directed General Winfield Scott to assist Virginia slaveholders seeking runaway slaves. But, in less than a month, Congress passed the first Confiscation Act providing that runaway slaves who had been used to aid the Confederacy could be granted freedom once they were under Union Army control.

As General Sherman pressed his attack down the South Carolina coast, he was directed to use former slaves as laborers and in any other way he might "deem most beneficial to the service; this, however, not being a general arming of them for service." When Sherman was transferred, he was replaced by an abolitionist officer, General David Hunter. Faced with an acute manpower shortage, and after pleading with Washington for reinforcements, General Hunter organized an all-Negro regiment, the First South Carolina Volunteers. Later, he was forced to disband most of the regiment, although one company remained on active duty.

On July 17, 1862, Congress passed a second Confiscation Act granting freedom to all slaves held by masters supporting the Confederacy. Five days after the Union victory at Antietam on September 22, 1862, President Lincoln issued a preliminary Emancipation Proclamation. Shortly thereafter, General B. F. Butler organized the First Regiment Louisiana Heavy Artillery, an all-Negro unit. The War Department then authorized organization of the first all-Negro regular army combat units; the first activated were the Massachusetts Fifty-fourth and Fifty-fifth Infanty Regiments. By the end of the

Drawing depicting the emancipation of the Negroes, highlighting
scenes from their past life and the new life of freedom.
(Schomburg Collection, New York Public Library)

war, there were approximately one hundred and fifty all-Negro regiments in the Union Army.

The final Emancipation Proclamation on January 1, 1863, proclaimed "all persons held as slaves within any State, or designated part of the State, the people whereof shall be in rebellion against the United States, shall be then, thenceforward, and forever free." It should be noted that the 1863 Proclamation contained no provisions not already provided for by Congress in the Confiscation Act of 1862. However, bearing the signature of the President and being his sole act,

it was of tremendous psychological importance. The Proclamation was issued as an Executive Order, but it became the law of the land with the ratification of the Thirteenth Amendment to the Constitution on December 18, 1865.

The Negro in the Union Army

With the draft act then in operation, 1863 saw the recruitment of Negro soldiers into the Union Army under the desig-

Training of Negro soldiers began immediately after promulgation of a provisional Emancipation Proclamation in 1862.
(Schomburg Collection, New York Public Library)

nation *United States Colored Troops,* or USCT. The majority of USCT's were commanded by white officers, many of whom resented their assignments. Before the war ended, however, approximately seventy-five Negroes had been commissioned as officers and served in the field. One of the most famous Negro officers was Lt. Col. William Reed, who lost his life during a charge of Confederate positions during the battle of Olustree, Florida.

While Negroes had fought for the Union in 1863, it was not until a year later that Congress granted black soldiers the same pay as white troops. The two Massachusetts regiments were so angered by the pay discrimination that they refused all money until their pay was made equal to that of their white comrades-in-arms. Time and again the Negro soldiers proved themselves brave and competent fighting men. When General Grant attacked Petersburg, a brigade of Negro troops over-ran the Confederate rifle pits. At the battle of Port Hudson, during the Mississippi Valley campaign, General Banks praised the Negro soldiers: "Their conduct was heroic; no troops could be more determined or more daring." Captain Matthew Miller gave this account of the Negro troops who fought at the battle of Milliken's Bend: "So they fought and died, defending the cause that we revere. They met death coolly, bravely; nor rashly did they expose themselves, but all were steady and obedient to orders."

When Confederate troops captured Negro Union soldiers, the black men rarely were treated as prisoners-of-war. If they were not killed on the spot, they were taken as slaves. On April 12, 1864, General Nathan Forrest and his Confederate troops captured the Union stronghold at Fort Pillow, forty miles north of Memphis, Tennessee. Half the garrison consisted of Negro troops, and the rebels ruthlessly killed every Negro they found.

By the end of the war, 200,000 Negroes had served in the Union Army and more than 38,000 had given their lives. The Congressional Medal of Honor, created during the Civil War as this nation's highest military award for valor in combat against an armed enemy, was awarded to twenty-two Negro soldiers.

Joseph T. Wilson wrote a complete account of Negro
participation in two important United States conflicts.
(Schomburg Collection, New York Public Library)

The War Ends

The Civil War finally ended at Appomattox Courthouse in central Virginia on April 9, 1865. The terms of the surrender were not vindictive, although the harsh realities of defeat lay heavily upon the mind of the Southerner. The Southern armies were disbanded, and the men were sent back to their homes to face the new social and political challenges that lay before them. There were, of course, some voices in the North that cried out for vengeance against the "treason and rebellion" of the South. For the most part, however, sanity and a desire to restore the South to full status in the Union prevailed among the responsible government leaders in Washington. In spite of a popular demand for his life, Jefferson Davis, the Confederate President, was not hanged. In fact, he was never even brought to trial.

There were *no* harsh and protracted war trials followed by a mass imprisonment of war criminals. Henry Wirz, superintendent of the Confederate prison at Andersonville, Georgia, was the only Confederate to lose his life for crimes committed during the war.

The conflict had irrevocably settled two issues: the Union was to remain intact; the slaves were to be free. The political integrity of the United States and the principle of inherent inviolability of human freedom had been established for all time.

Beyond the restoration of the Union and the emancipation of the slaves, however, there was little agreement among the various Northern and Southern factions on what should be done now. When, and in what manner might seceded states regain their political sovereignty? What was to be done about the status of the ex-slaves? How was the Southern economy to be rebuilt in the absence of slave labor?

The North had won the war, the Union had been preserved, and the South had come to the end of an era.

Long before the final Confederate surrender, President Lincoln had decided on a plan for reconstructing the nation. With the exception of high Confederate officials, Lincoln intended to grant general amnesty to Southerners, asking merely that they swear future allegiance to the United States. When one tenth of a state's 1860 electorate had taken such an oath and established a government consistent with the Emancipation Proclamation, Lincoln planned to recognize the state; then, it would be readmitted to the Union. Negroes were to be excluded from participating in the political reconstruction, but the President planned the creation of Federal agencies that would handle the needs of black men and women. As a general rule, the President did not intend to give Negroes the vote, although he was known to favor enfranchising a limited number of Negroes who were either property owners or had distinguished war records.

Many members of Congress felt that Lincoln's reconstruction plan was far too lenient. Congress responded by passing its own blueprint, the Wade-Davis Act, in July, 1864. The Wade-Davis Act provided that an oath of *past* as well as *future* loyalty be taken; an "ironclad" oath that arms had not been voluntarily borne against the Union. The President vetoed the Wade-Davis Act because he felt it rejected "the Christian principles of forgiveness on terms of repentance."

When Andrew Johnson became President after Lincoln's murder, the Tennessee Republican proceeded to implement his predecessor's reconstruction plan. Once again Congress rebelled and appointed a Joint Committee on Reconstruction whose first task was to add to the force of the Emancipation Proclamation. The Proclamation, a wartime measure issued by the President as "an act of military necessity," merely freed those slaves in states rebelling against the Federal government. The Thirteenth Amendment to the Constitution (the first of the so-called "Civil War Amendments") abolished slavery throughout the nation.

Citizenship and Southern Reaction

Negroes finally became citizens of the United States on July 28, 1868, with the ratification of the Fourteenth Amendment to the Constitution. But while that Amendment was awaiting ratification, the South moved to re-shackle the Negro with a series of "Black Codes."

The Codes established an interlocking system of social, economic, and political controls aimed at placing the Negro in a position below that of any white person in the general population. The Codes dealt with apprenticeships, labor contracts, migration, vagrancy, civil and legal rights. Freedmen without lawful employment were declared vagrants; they were not allowed to purchase or lease land except in incorporated cities; they could not enter any occupation except that of farmer or servant without a special license. In effect, the Black Codes implied that Negroes were to be a supporting caste, both economically and psychologically, for the defeated South.

Congress moved rapidly against the Black Codes and enacted a Civil Rights Act in 1866. The law granted Federal protection to the Negro in a variety of social situations, and was also intended to protect him against physical violence. President Johnson vetoed the legislation, but Congress overrode his veto.

In March, 1867, Congress passed the First Reconstruction Act aimed at defeating the conservative reconstruction policies of President Johnson. The act provided for military rule in the South until such time as individual Southern states met certain political conditions. The Southern states were divided into five military districts and the state governments already recognized by Johnson were abolished. New elections were called to fill state offices. Congress declared that no state could be represented in the national legislature or be returned to civilian control until a duly elected state convention ratified the "Civil War Amendments" to the Constitution; tied to that provision was the additional requirement that Negroes be given the vote. Those Southerners who had held high military or political positions in the Confederacy were barred from taking active roles in the state conventions.

Negroes as Lawmakers

Of the 1,330,000 voters registering under the Reconstruction Acts, 703,000 were Negroes and only 627,000 were whites. The Negro majority happened because many whites could not take an oath that they had not given aid and comfort to enemies of the United States. But Negroes did hold population majorities in Alabama, Louisiana, Mississippi, Florida, and South Carolina. The new laws also benefitted "poor whites" who, for the first time, were freed of restrictive property qualifications and were able to register and vote.

Two Negroes, Blanche K. Bruce and Hiram R. Revels, were elected United States Senators from Mississippi. Between 1869 and 1880, a total of twenty-two Negroes served as members of the House of Representatives. The elections conducted under the Reconstruction Acts also sent several Negroes to high public office in Southern state governments. Francis L. Cordozo became Treasurer of South Carolina; J. C. Gibbs was elected Secretary of the State of Florida, and Pinkney B. Pinchback served briefly as Governor of Louisiana. Negroes were also elected to state legislatures; in South Carolina they constituted the majority in the lower house, while whites retained control of the Senate.

Some Negroes elected to state offices were both illiterate and incompetent, for it had been illegal to educate a slave. Consequently, some freedmen lacked the education and experience to fulfill their duties as lawmakers. However, the overall quality of Negro legislators in state houses appears to have been quite high. One indication is that state constitutions written by the so-called "Black Reconstruction" governments remained in force long after 1876, when Negroes and Radical Republicans lost power. The South Carolina constitution of 1868 was not rewritten until 1895; Mississippi did not adopt a new constitution until 1890; and the Virginia constitution remained in force from 1870 until 1902.

Real Control and Power

The majority of local, state, and Federal officials were not Negroes, but Southern whites. Some whites—adventurers who became known as "carpetbaggers"—came from the North to make financial profit from the defeated South. Generally, the Northern carpetbaggers had little concern for either the Southern whites or the Negroes, although they were able to count upon Negro votes by passing themselves off as "Northern friends." The carpetbaggers were joined in their exploitative practices by some white Southerners, known in the South as "scalawags." The two groups dominated local governments while selfishly lining their pockets with corruption-stained cash.

The Struggle to Learn

Realizing that education was the greatest need if Negroes were to realize the benefits of their freedom and have any lasting role in the nation's political affairs, "Black Reconstruction" legislatures concentrated on public education. South Carolina led the states of the Old Confederacy providing free public education for both white and Negro children. Other states where Negroes were politically powerful followed South Carolina's example.

Hundreds of white teachers from the North journeyed

The first Negro Senator and Representatives were elected to the 41st and 42nd Congress of the United States.
(Schomburg Collection, New York Public Library)

South to establish and staff schools, academies, seminaries, and colleges. An Army officer, General O. O. Howard, head of the Freedmen's Bureau, founded Howard University in Washington, D. C. Many of today's leading Negro colleges and universities are products of combined white and Negro dedication to education. Some of the schools founded during the Reconstruction period are: Fisk University, Nashville, Tennessee; Atlanta University, Atlanta, Georgia; Hampton Institute in Virginia; Talladega College in Alabama; Tougaloo College in Mississippi; Morgan College in Baltimore, Maryland; Knoxville College in Knoxville, Tennessee; and Tuskegee Institute in Alabama.

By 1870, approximately 150,000 Negroes were enrolled in Southern schools, taught by 3,500 teachers. Many of the students attended classes at night with candles or oil lamps, more often than not, the only illumination. Twenty years later, one million Negro children were the pupils of 25,000 Negro teachers who had been trained by white instructors from the North. Many white teachers were suspected by the Southerners of teaching social equality to Negro students. As a result, a large number of schools were burned and the teachers forced to return North. This was not true in every section of the South. In cities such as Baltimore, Richmond, and New Orleans, Southern white women taught Negro children and encouraged them to aspire to higher stations in life.

The Problem of Earning a Living

While vast numbers of freed Negroes hungered for an education, they were faced with the more immediate problem of earning a living. The Freedmen's Bureau Act, passed over President Johnson's veto in 1866, provided for the assignment of confiscated Southern land to Negroes. But Mr. Johnson's policy of restoring the lands to white ex-Confederates nullified the act's provisions. Furthermore, Reconstruction left the whites with land, but without either money or labor to develop it. Since Northern bankers had investment capital, and Negro labor was abundant, the major question facing the South was how to bring together the land, the money, and the labor in an economically profitable enterprise.

Many new schools were set up for teaching the freed Negroes, both young and old, during the Reconstruction period. (*The Bettmann Archive*)

Howard University was chartered by the government in 1867 for the advanced education of Negro youth.
(Schomburg Collection, New York Public Library)

Sharecropping was the South's answer to the problem. The financiers lent the farmers money and the farmers, in turn, used it to purchase tools, seed, and food for the Negro workers. Sharecropping bound Negro families to the land and to white landowners almost as effectively as had slavery. The landowner took a lien against the tenant farmer's share of the crop; the lien was security for the landowner's investment of seed, livestock, and food. When accounts were settled after harvest, the sharecropper (theoretically, at least) was supposed to "share" the profits that remained after the crop was sold. In fact, the usually illiterate tenant always found that his account was "overdrawn"—he had been advanced more for food, clothing, and other necessities than his share of the harvest was worth. As a result, he found himself in debt to the landowner. To wipe out the debt, the tenant was required to make a crop for the same landowner the next year. By the time the second year's crop was harvested, the tenant was usually more hopelessly in debt than before. If a tenant tried to leave the farm without paying off his "debt," he and his family could be (and often were) jailed and fined. The fines were paid by sending the tenant back to the *same* farm to work off the fine—usually at less than a dollar a day.

Much of today's present race problem in the South has its roots in the Reconstruction period, and especially in the creation of the sharecropper class. The poor whites, who had generally lived in the hills and on the less productive lands adjacent to the plantations, found their traditionally marginal incomes reduced still further after the Civil War. The postwar competition for jobs on the farms, in the building trades and elsewhere, increased the bitterness and resentment between the poor whites and Negroes.

Even before the war, competition between Negro artisans and mechanics and their poor white counterparts had become acute. In 1845, the Georgia legislature barred the making of contracts with Negro mechanics—slave or free. In spite of such attempts to restrict their employment, skilled Negroes in Charleston, New Orleans and other cities, held a virtual monopoly in the mechanical trades. In Virginia, some former slaves worked in the production of cotton textiles, tobacco, iron, and flour. Of the 120,000 artisans in the South at the end of the war, 100,000 were Negroes. They were employed as gunsmiths, plasterers, cabinetmakers, blacksmiths, masons, riverboat pilots, and engineers.

Carpetbaggers—Northern adventurers—flocked to the South to make money and seize power during the Reconstruction period. *(The Bettmann Archive)*

The Rise of Segregation

Slavery had been justified in the South on both theological and sociological grounds; segregation's excuse was purely biological. The segregationists believed that the Negro's biological inferiority made him incapable of intellectual, artistic, or moral achievement.

Segregation was developed by white America as a means of insuring social, political, and economic distance between the races. To keep the Negro subservient, it was necessary to keep him poor and uneducated. But, at the same time, the Negro's labor was necessary to the restoration of the South's economy.

Ironically, the preservation of segregation became the special function of the poor white, who had traditionally been as victimized by the prevailing economic, social, and political

Klansmen walk down a main street in Raleigh, North Carolina.
(National Urban League)

conditions as the Negro. For segregation presented the poor white with a psychological release so strong that he simply overlooked the common lot he shared with the Negro. Awarded social certification as the Negro's superior, the poor white flaunted the "white supremacy" code because it artificially raised his position in society.

The Ku Klux Klan

While almost every Southern institution was committed to the white supremacy doctrine, it was the Ku Klux Klan which became the most notorious organization in the doctrine's enforcement. The Klan was organized at Pulaski, Tennessee, in 1865, by Confederate General Nathan B. Forrest, a former slave trader. The Klan allegedly began as a social club with certain distinctive ritualistic costumes, but it was soon discovered that the Klan's mysterious hooded white robes intimidated Negroes. Composed largely of lower-class whites, the Klan ironically became the self-appointed preserver of "the Southern way of life" as it had been envisioned by the white aristocracy. Operating mainly as night-riding terrorists, the Klan thrived on violence: floggings, lynchings, arson, and murder. Congress finally enacted a series of "Force Laws" aimed directly at the Klan, but the organization continued to operate. Between 1870 and 1900, thousands of whites were arrested for Klan butchery, and more than 1,200 were convicted. Still the Klan functioned openly, until it had accomplished its primary goals of reducing the Negro vote and restoring control of Southern governments to whites. The original Klan finally faded, only to rear its ugly head again in the twentieth century.

Reconstruction Ends With a Deal

The Presidential election of 1876 was the death knell of Reconstruction. The Democratic candidate, New York Governor Samuel J. Tilden, had earned a reputation as a vigorous

The Hampton Trade Institute in Virginia was one of the few good, if not exceptional schools that Negroes attended.
(Collection, The Museum of Modern Art, New York. Gift of Lincoln Kirstein.)

reformer by breaking the vicious "Boss Tweed" ring in New York City. His opponent, Republican Governor Rutherford B. Hayes of Ohio, had served as a Congressman and as a Major General in the Union Army during the Civil War.

The election returns from Oregon, Florida, Louisiana, and South Carolina were disputed almost as soon as they were counted. Since the Constitution did not provide for such a contingency, a Congressional Commission was created to settle the matter. Hayes was declared the winner by a margin of one electoral vote (185 to 184 for Tilden). Before assuming office, President-elect Hayes assured the Democrats that if they would not contest the election decision of the Commission, he would withdraw the remaining Northern troops from the South when he entered the White House. Hayes kept his part of the deal, and with Union soldiers gone, Southern whites immediately removed all Negroes from public office.

The Courts Sanction Segregation

The Negro's "place" in society became a matter of law in every Southern state during the 1890's. But the long legal history of racial discrimination and segregation in the United States antedates the Civil War.

One of the earliest trials involving the issue of segregation arose in the North in the 1849 case of *Roberts v. City of Boston*. A Negro girl tried to enter an all-white school in Boston, where a local ordinance provided for the segregation of white and Negro pupils. Boston lawyer Charles Sumner, later to become a famous legislator, argued for the plaintiff that the Massachusetts constitution, in declaring all men to be free and equal, meant that all men (and women, for that matter) were entitled to equal protection of the laws. The segregation of Negroes in separate schools, Sumner contended, violated the principle of equal protection, and deprived Negroes of their rights as defined in the state constitution. Sumner's argument was the first in which the concept of equal protection under law was introduced into a racial controversy.

The Massachusetts Supreme Court ruled in favor of the City of Boston. The court held that segregation did not in itself constitute discrimination, and that, if caste distinction is created or increased by segregated schools, it "is not created by *law* and probably cannot be changed by law."

Six years later, in 1855, the Massachusetts legislature

passed a law prohibiting segregation in the public schools. But the damage had been done as far as the Negro was concerned. *Roberts v. City of Boston* had been established as a legal precedent for similar cases across the land. Following the Civil War, state-enforced segregation received court approval in New York, Ohio, Missouri, California, and various other states outside the South.

Plessy v. Ferguson (1896) was the first racial-segregation case decided by the United States Supreme Court. Homer Plessy was seven eighths white and one eighth Negro; he charged that a Louisiana statute, requiring segregation on trains within the state, violated rights granted him by the Thirteenth and Fourteenth Amendments to the Constitution. Plessy's main argument was a warning that if a physical distinction, such as color of skin, could be used as a basis for segregation, then discrimination against blondes and redheads could also be considered reasonable and legal. Furthermore, argued Plessy, in providing legal sanction for the segregation of some of its citizens, Louisiana implied that such citizens were inferior.

In an 8-1 decision, the Court denied that segregation by race necessarily implied racial inferiority. Declaring the case to be reduced to a "question of whether the statute of Louisiana [was] a reasonable regulation," the Court held that for a legislature to act in conformity with "established usages, customs, and traditions of a people . . . and the preservation of the public peace and good order" was, in fact, "reasonable." As might have been expected, the Court cited as a precedent the earlier case of *Roberts v. City of Boston*.

Associate Justice John Marshall Harlan dissented: "In the view of the Constitution . . . there is in this country no superior, dominant, ruling class of citizens. There is no caste here. Our Constitution is color-blind. In respect of civil rights, all citizens are equal before the law." But the Court's decision in *Plessy v. Ferguson* established the "separate but equal" doctrine that remained a legal guidepost until May 17, 1954.

The Supreme Court's view on matters of state's rights affecting the Negro was evident even prior to the decision in *Plessy v. Ferguson*. It began with the *Slaughterhouse Cases,* 83 U. S. 36 (1873); the cases hung on an interpretation of the "due process" clause of the Fourteenth Amendment. In 1869, the Louisiana legislature granted the Crescent City Live-Stock Landing and Slaughter House Company the exclusive privilege of slaughtering animals in the New Orleans area.

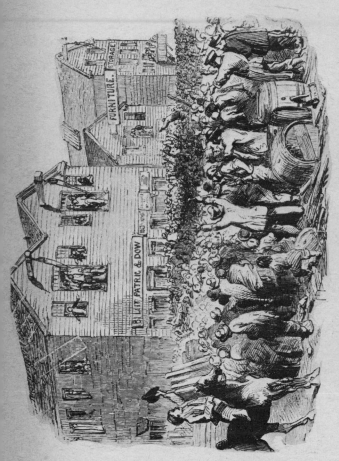

A lynching in San Francisco. (*Picture Collection, New York Public Library*)

STATE	NUMBER OF LYNCHINGS *	**	Total
Alabama	116	16	132
Arizona	1	3	4
Arkansas	115	12	127
California	10	2	12
Colorado	6	1	7
Connecticut	—	—	—
Delaware	1	—	1
District of Columbia	—	—	—
Florida	141	29	170
Georgia	240	62	302
Idaho	2	—	2
Illinois	12	1	13
Indiana	7	1	8
Iowa	2	1	3
Kansas	8	—	8
Kentucky	58	10	68
Louisiana	145	27	172
Maine	—	—	—
Maryland	6	—	6
Massachusetts	—	—	—
Michigan	—	1	1
Minnesota	3	—	3
Mississippi	217	68	285
Missouri	40	1	41
Montana	8	1	9

STATE	NUMBER OF LYNCHINGS *	**	Total
Nebraska	2	1	3
Nevada	2	1	3
New Hampshire	—	—	—
New Jersey	—	—	—
New Mexico	5	1	6
New York	—	—	—
North Carolina	35	—	35
North Dakota	2	3	5
Ohio	5	—	5
Oklahoma	38	10	48
Oregon	1	3	4
Pennsylvania	1	—	1
Rhode Island	—	—	—
South Carolina	63	8	71
South Dakota	1	1	2
Tennessee	73	3	76
Texas	181	21	201
Utah	1	—	1
Vermont	—	—	—
Virginia	25	1	26
Washington	1	1	2
West Virginia	12	1	13
Wisconsin	1	—	1
Wyoming	8	1	9
TOTAL	1595	291	1886

* Exact location known.
** Exact location unknown.

Table of Lynchings by states during the period from 1900 to 1931, according to data elaborated by Tuskegee Institute's Research Department.

The local butchers charged that their "property" (that is, their right to labor) had been taken from them by the terms of the charter. In a 5-4 decision, the Court held that the "due process" clause only granted protection of *national* citizenship rights, but did not throw a mantle of protection over state citizenship rights. The decision weighed heavily upon the Negro, because the states exercised control over such matters as public transportation and education.

Another Supreme Court interpretation adversely affecting Negroes was *United States v. Cruikshank*, 92 U. S. 552 (1876). In that decision, the Court refused to punish persons who had broken up a Negro meeting at which a forthcoming Louisiana election was being discussed. The Court held that breaking up such a meeting could only be a crime if the meeting had been concerned with a National election.

Yet another court decision restrained the emancipated Negro. In the *Civil Rights Cases*, 109 U. S. 3 (1883), the sections of the 1875 Civil Rights Act prohibiting racial discrimination in places of public accommodation were struck down by an 8-1 decision. Again, Mr. Justice Harlan was the lone dissenter.

The South interpreted *Plessy v. Ferguson* as judicial approval for the complete separation of the races in every aspect of public life. Schools, trains, buses, public buildings, parks, playgrounds, beaches, waiting rooms, water fountains —none could be used jointly by Negroes and whites. The South did make some effort to make provision for Negroes, but it could not realistically expect its truncated economy to support a completely duplicate system of public facilities and institutions. Negroes were provided with some schools and public libraries, but they were admittedly inferior and were seldom, if ever, "equal" to corresponding facilities provided for whites. Public auditoriums, fairgrounds, exhibition halls, were often set aside for the exclusive use of Negroes at certain times of the year. It was a common practice in most Southern cities to permit Negroes to attend the public zoo on one afternoon each week. All this was considered legal and adequate within the "separate but equal" doctrine laid down by the Court in *Plessy v. Ferguson*.

New Philosophies and New Directions

Just a few months before the decision in *Plessy v. Ferguson*, the most prominent Negro in America took a position that appeared to condone the philosophy of racial segregation. It happened during the 1895 Cotton States International Exposition in Atlanta, Georgia. Booker T. Washington, founder of Tuskegee Institute, set forth what has been called ever since the "separate fingers doctrine," in which he called upon his race to concentrate on gaining material advantages through work rather than social equality through agitation or militancy.

To many people, it seemed that Washington had settled for all time the issue of the "proper" relationship between whites and Negroes. In his speech, Washington asserted that Negroes and whites could subsist equally and simultaneously as each finger on a hand; therefore, whites need not fear independent Negro progress. The view was widely praised in the national press, and Booker T. Washington was hailed by many whites as a rational and reliable Negro spokesman.

Meanwhile, an increasingly vocal segment of Negro leadership contended that the full rights of citizenship guaranteed by the Constitution could not be realized within the narrow confines of Washington's theory. In 1898, the dream of peaceful relations between the races in the South was rudely challenged by a widespread outbreak of racial violence. Riots, lynchings, and the progressive disenfranchisement of Negroes darkened the closing of the nineteenth and the opening of the twentieth century. Little by little, Washington's philosophy was repudiated as weaknesses began to show in the fabric of his argument. It became increasingly evident to his foremost critics that only the efficacy of the law—fairly administered to all citizens—could protect the Negro minority and insure its full participation in every aspect of American life.

Thirty prominent Negroes, led by Dr. W. E. B. DuBois, met on July 29, 1905, at Fort Erie, Canada, in the interest of "aggressive action on the part of men who believe in Negro freedom and growth." They founded an organization known as the "Niagara Movement," a group that evolved, by 1909, into the National Association for the Advancement of Colored People—the NAACP.

ʀractically stripped of political power and without hope of an improved social atmosphere, the Southern Negro entered the twentieth century looking toward the North as a long-sought promised land. Nearly eighty per cent of America's Negro population still lived in the eleven states that had comprised the Confederacy during the Civil War. Those Negroes were largely unskilled and, as a consequence, their employment was generally limited to common labor, domestic service, and sharecropping. Many of those who went North found themselves competing with European immigrants for the most menial jobs.

The forces of nature also helped push the Negro off the Southern farms and toward the industrialized North. In 1915 and 1916, the cotton plantations were severely hit by swarms of boll weevils; then floods came and doomed the harvests. As World War I drained away America's youth and European immigration was cut off, labor recruiters from the North went South to recruit Negroes to work in the defense plants, ship-yards, steel mills, and packing houses. With railroad tickets in their pockets and glowing reports of freedom in the North to entice the hungry and oppressed Negroes, the recruiters helped thousands leave the South. For the first time in their memory, Southern Negroes were being "courted" by whites; they accepted the promises and headed North. The Negro population of Northern cities increased quite rapidly in the first twenty years of the twentieth century: New York City by 91,000; Philadelphia by 73,000; Detroit by 36,000; and Chi-cago by 79,000.

The masses of Negroes flocking to the North were not ab-sorbed easily. The military demands of World War I drew heavily upon the nation's manpower, and the vacant jobs left behind were frequently filled by Negroes. For those white workers who remained in their jobs, the Negro migration seemed to present a clear competitive challenge. At the same time, the Ku Klux Klan was re-emerging as a device of terror aimed at Negroes, Catholics, and Jews. Lynchings and flog-gings were once more frequent occurrences. In the year 1900 alone, more than a hundred Negroes were lynched. By 1914, that gruesome figure had risen to eleven hundred.

With the death of Booker T. Washington in 1915, the Ne-gro population found itself without a major spokesman at a moment when one was sorely needed. The void of personal leadership was slowly filled by a new institution, the Negro press. Negro newspapers performed the dual role of exposing racial discrimination and of bolstering morale. Perhaps the most dramatic example of Negro journalism in this century is *The Chicago Defender,* founded by Robert S. Abbott.

Abbott was the son of a Georgia slave who, after the Emancipation, operated a small grocery store. After Abbott's father died, his mother married John H. Sengstacke, a clergy-man of German and Negro parentage. Sengstacke was an energetic man. He devoted much of his spare time to teaching school and editing a small newspaper on which his stepson, young Robert Abbott, assisted. When it first appeared in 1905, *The Chicago Defender* was a relatively crude one-sheet hand-bill. Later, Abbott decided to experiment, and the paper fea-tured bold headlines and news stories about the so-called "average man." *The Defender* was one of the main voices en-couraging Negroes to leave the South, and Abbott made it clear that he considered World War I a tremendous oppor-

In 1917, 15,000 Negroes marched down Fifth Avenue, New York City, to protest race riot killings in Texas, Tennessee and Missouri. *(Schomburg Collection, New York Public Library)*

tunity for his people. An example of that conviction appeared in *The Defender's* editorial of January 9, 1915:

> It [the war] has meant that the thousands who a year ago were dependent upon charity are today employed and making a comfortable living for themselves and their families. The colored man and woman are, and must be for some years to come, laborers. There is no line of endeavor that we cannot fit ourselves for. These same factories, mills and workshops that have been closed to us, through necessity are being opened to us. We are to be given a chance, not through choice but because it is expedient. Prejudice vanishes when the almighty dollar is on the wrong side of the balance sheet. Give the best that is in us when we answer the call. It is significant that the great west is calling to the Southern black man to leave his old home and come out here where the prospects are bright for the future. Slowly but surely all over this country we are gradually edging in first this and then that place, getting a foothold before making a place for our brother. By this only can the so-called race problems be solved. It is merely a question of a better and a closer understanding between the races. We are Americans and must live together, so why not live in peace?

The threat of vast numbers of Negro workers leaving the South forced many white businessmen to try to stop the exodus. In a few Southern cities, joint white and Negro conferences were held and the whites even promised reforms to improve the Negro's lot. But Abbott scorned the white South's promises of reform in *The Defender's* editorial of October 7, 1916:

> Turn a deaf ear to everybody. You see they are not lifting their laws to help you, are they? Have they stopped their Jim Crow cars? Can you buy a Pullman sleeper where you wish? Will they give you a square deal in court yet? Once upon a time we permitted other people to think for us—today we are thinking and acting for ourselves with the result that our "friends" are getting alarmed at our progress. We'd like to oblige these unselfish (?) souls and remain slaves in the South, but to their section of the country we have said, as the song goes, "I hear you calling me," and have boarded the train singing, "Good-bye, Dixie Land."

While he was urging Southern Negroes to move North, Abbott was also establishing *The Defender* as a permanent institution, a voice for those Negroes who heeded his plea. Since there were few trained Negro journalists available, Abbott built his editorial staff from promising but otherwise inexperienced men and women. The late novelist Willard Motley started his writing career on *The Defender,* as did Gwen-

Even today, more than a million migrant agricultural workers follow planting, cultivating, harvesting and processing jobs from one part of the country to another. *(NAACP)*

dolyn Brooks, the only Negro woman ever to win a Pulitzer
Prize. After Abbott's death in 1940, his nephew, John H.
Sengstacke, became *The Defender's* editor and publisher. In
February, 1956, Sengstacke launched *The Chicago Daily De-
fender* which, with *The Atlanta World,* is one of the nation's
two Negro daily newspapers.

Although *The Defender* led the way, other Negro newspapers also grew and prospered during the great migration:
*The New York Age; The Cleveland Gazette; The Philadel-
phia Tribune; The Richmond Planet; The Dallas Express;
The Atlanta Independent; The St. Louis Argus; The Pitts-
burgh Courier; The Norfolk Journal and Guide;* and *The
Baltimore Afro-American.*

World War I

When the United States entered World War I on April 6,
1917, approximately 10,000 Negroes were already serving in
the Regular Army. Almost immediately, the War Department
stopped accepting Negro volunteers; the Marine Corps and
Coast Guard followed suit. The Navy established what was to
become a quarter-century-long policy of limiting Negroes to
service in menial assignments, usually as mess attendants.

The passage of the Selective Service Act reopened Negro
inductions into the Army as enlisted men. But the services
made no provisions for the training and appointment of Negroes as commissioned officers. Indeed, the Army sought to
remove its lone Negro West Point graduate from the active
list.

Charles Young graduated from the United States Military
Academy as a second lieutenant and a Bachelor of Science
on August 31, 1889. He served as a cavalry officer in Cuba,
Mexico, Haiti, and Liberia. On one occasion, white soldiers
refused to salute the Negro officer. Young removed his jacket
and ordered them to salute his grade insignia. By the time
this country entered World War I, Young had become a full
colonel and in 1917, had he not been a Negro, probably
would have been promoted to brigadier general. But suddenly
the War Department found that Colonel Young suffered from
"high blood pressure" and must be retired. The colonel decided to contest the Army's diagnosis and demonstrated his
physical fitness for active duty by riding horseback from Wil-
berforce, Ohio, to Washington, D. C., a distance of 350 miles.

In spite of that performance, the Army retired him. Eventually, after many protests from Negroes, Colonel Young was recalled to active duty and given staff assignments, first in Illinois and later in Liberia, where he died.

The impersonal treatment of Colonel Young impelled Negro leaders to press the government for officer-training programs for qualified Negro candidates. As a result of the continuing pressure, an all-Negro officers training school was established at Fort Des Moines, Iowa, with the commandant's position given to a white colonel. On October 15, 1917, 639 Negroes received commissions; 106 were appointed captains, the remainder either first or second lieutenants. Later, other Negro officers were commissioned.

Nearly half of the 100,000 Negroes who served in France were assigned to labor duty, either handling cargo or building railroads and bridges. Most Negro soldiers who saw combat duty were assigned to the 92nd or 93rd Infantry Divisions. The all-Negro 369th Infantry Regiment received the French *Croix de Guerre* for gallantry at Maison-en-Champagne, and was cited for bravery on eleven separate occasions. A Negro enlisted man of the 369th, Private Henry Johnson of Albany, New York, was the first American decorated by the French with the *Croix de Guerre*. Nicknamed the "Hell Fighters" by the Germans, the 369th was the first Allied combat unit to cross the Rhine River into Germany. In all, 171 officers and men of the regiment were decorated for combat bravery. Another all-Negro regiment, the 8th Infantry from Illinois, received more combat citations than any other American regiment in France.

The Red Summer

While Negroes were either serving in France or working in the nation's war plants, some Americans were creating *de facto* segregation or "Black Ghettos" at home. Housing restrictions against Negroes usually began with white rental agents, but the restrictions were widely supported by local municipal authorities. There were two usual patterns in the establishment of segregated Negro areas in Northern cities: Either Negro families slowly filtered into previously all-white areas, or there was what many whites described as an "invasion" of the neighborhoods by Negroes. Such "invaded" neighborhoods were traditionally low-rent areas, situated close

to industrial plants. When the number of Negroes in a neighborhood reached, or appeared to be reaching, parity with
whites, the whites usually moved away and left the area en-
tirely Negro.

By the time World War I ended, some Northerners, as well
as Southerners, had become openly hostile to the Negro on
two major fronts: housing and jobs. Being the "last hired,"
the Negro came to expect (as was too often true) that he was
the "first fired." It was not quite so easy to displace Negroes
from residential areas. A pattern of mysterious bombings directed against Negro property began to take shape in many
Northern cities. Some white real estate men who sold or
rented property to Negroes became bomb targets themselves.

In the last six months of 1919, more than twenty race
riots rocked the United States. The Negro poet, James Weldon Johnson, described the months as "The Red Summer,"
and the redness was the blood of whites and Negroes that
flowed in the streets of American cities.

Throughout the period of racial stress, hundreds of Negroes lost their lives over the false issue of rape and the
myth of their aggressiveness. The riots of 1919, particularly
the one in Washington, D. C., illustrated the extent of this
fallacy. It is no fallacy that the Negro male had to live with
the constant fear of lynching.

The bloodiest and longest race riot of 1919 occurred in
Chicago. It began on a hot July afternoon when a young Negro boy swam into a Lake Michigan beach area that was
restricted to whites. The whites attacked the youngster with
stones and, unable to swim through the barrage, the boy
drowned. Pitched battles between whites and Negroes followed for thirteen days, with mobs of both races raging
through the city. Thirty-eight persons died and 537 were
wounded during the melee. In addition, more than one thousand families (mostly Negro) were made homeless before
the Illinois National Guard restored order in the Windy City.

Marcus Garvey

After 1919, social and political development for the Negro
masses was championed by traditional Negro organizations
such as the NAACP and the Urban League which pressed
campaigns to obtain civil rights and increase employment.
However, those organizations lacked the emotional appeal

the masses found in Marcus Garvey's Universal Negro Improvement Association. Garvey, a British West Indian, advocated "back to Africa" as the *only* solution for the American Negro. He reasoned that white Americans would never treat their Negro fellow citizens justly. By 1923, Garvey claimed six million members in UNIA, but more cautious estimates placed the membership at slightly over a half million. Garvey's most spectacular accomplishment was the organization of the Black Star Steamship Lines. The line was to provide a triangular service between New York City, the West Indies, and Africa. In one two-year period it was reported that he raised over ten million dollars. He had built his organization into a multi-million concern, but he himself had no business or financial acumen whatever. In 1925, he was indicted and convicted of using the mails to defraud. This was, however, possibly the fault of pressure placed on him by Negro leaders. After serving two years in the U. S. Penitentiary at Atlanta, Georgia, he was deported to his native Jamaica where he was elected to public office in Kingston. Although removed from participation in American life, Garvey continued to be a popular symbol among Negroes until his death in 1940 at the age of fifty-three.

Employment

When the stock market crash of October 1929 brought the Great Depression to white America, many Negroes had already become veterans of poverty. By the time the depression had taken a firm grip on the nation, Negroes were deep in a discrimination-tainted desperation. Even those jobs that had been traditionally "Negro" were being taken by whites who would have scorned such work ten years earlier. A few statistics illustrate the situation. By the middle of June, 1934, 52.2 per cent of the Negroes in Northern cities were on relief rolls, while only 13.3 per cent of whites were receiving such assistance. Furthermore, the passage of some New Deal measures sponsored by the Roosevelt Administration had little effect on the plight of many Negroes. Few Negroes were eligible for coverage under the Social Security Act because in its original form the act did not cover domestic or agricultural workers. Thus, large numbers of black Americans were unable to receive either unemployment compensation or old-age benefits. Moreover, with state agencies administering the programs, Negroes in many Southern communities who *did* qualify were usually paid less than whites.

The Negro's economic condition has been particularly affected by his reception or rejection into the ranks of organized labor. The dominant labor organization at the turn of the century was the American Federation of Labor (AFL), led by Samuel Gompers. The AFL was organized strictly on a craft basis (electricians, carpenters, plumbers, etc.). Since the vast majority of Negro workers were either semi- or unskilled, they were excluded from membership in the AFL ranks. Negroes constituted only 6.4 per cent of the unskilled workers in the steel industry in 1910; ten years later, that percentage had risen to 17 per cent. In Chicago's meat-packing industry, only thirty-three of the 4,414 semi-skilled workers were Negroes in 1910; of 8,426 laborers in the stockyards, only thirty-four were Negroes. By 1920, there were 1,558 Negroes among the industry's 6,931 semi-skilled workers, and Negroes numbered 1,397 of the 7,032 laborers.

The Negro Joins Organized Labor

Two of the traditional menial jobs "reserved" for Negroes became the springboard for their organized entry into the American labor movement. Through the efforts of Asa Randolph and Willard Townsend the sleeping car porter and the redcap were unionized.

Asa Phillip Randolph grew up in Florida, where his father was a minister and his mother operated a small tailor shop. Young Randolph attended Cookman Institute in Daytona Beach and the City College of New York. He had trouble holding jobs in New York, mainly because of his habit of trying to unionize his fellow workers. In 1917, Randolph became an editor of *The Messenger,* a magazine whose editors offered, without apology, the following statement of position and intention:

> . . . . to appeal to reason, to lift our pens above the cringing demagogy of the times, and above the cheap peanut politics of the old reactionary Negro leaders. . . . Patriotism has no appeal to us; justice has. Party has no weight with us; principle has. Loyalty is meaningless; it depends on what one is loyal to. Prayer is not one of our remedies; it depends on what one is praying for.

Invited to organize the Brotherhood of Sleeping Car Porters and Maids in 1925, Randolph became the target of the railroads as well as the Negroes. Each was fearful that unionization would destroy what was, for both, a virtual monopoly. The pressures failed to discourage Randolph, and he eventually gained recognition for his union from the major rail lines.

Willard Townsend's granduncle was one of the founders of Ohio's Oberlin College. Townsend's youth was spent in Cincinnati, Ohio, where he lived in an unsegregated neighborhood and worked as a redcap at the Union station. A clerk in the Army during World War I, Townsend later completed his formal education at the Royal College of Science in Toronto, Canada. During his college days, he also worked for the Canadian Pacific Railroad. But jobs for Negro college graduates were scarce in the 1920's, and Townsend was forced to become a redcap once again, this time in Chicago. When the Wagner Labor Relations Act was passed in 1935, Townsend moved swiftly to organize the redcaps. When dissident members of the AFL (led by John L. Lewis of the United Mine Workers) split from that union to form the CIO (Congress of Industrial Organizations), Townsend took his United Transport Service Employees into the new organization. With Randolph leading the Pullman Porters, both men became nationally recognized labor leaders. Twenty years later, in 1955, when the CIO and the AFL decided to merge, both Randolph and Townsend became vice presidents of the AFL-CIO.

The CIO's liberal policies toward Negroes in the mid-thirties paid off for both the union and its Negro members. Between 1935 and 1945, Negro union membership (mainly in the CIO) jumped from 180,000 to 1,250,000. As World War II began in 1939, this country's need to arm itself created demands for additional workers in defense industries. However, racial discrimination threatened once again to slam the door of opportunity on America's Negroes. Randolph, Townsend, Walter White of the NAACP, and other Negro leaders warned that if President Roosevelt did not issue an Executive order banning racial discrimination, they would lead fifty thousand Negroes in a march on the nation's capital. The threat brought results. On June 25, 1941, the President issued Executive Order 8802 providing for anti-discrimination clauses in *all* defense contracts, and the establishment of a Fair Employment Practices Commission (FEPC) in the Office of Production Management. Subsequently, Executive or-

ders covering racial discrimination in industries with Federal contracts were issued by Presidents Truman, Eisenhower, Kennedy, and Johnson. World War II was actually the turning point for the American Negro's economic advancement. Between 1940 and 1944, Negro male skilled workers increased from 4.4 per cent to 7.3 per cent; the increase in the semi-skilled category was from 12 per cent to 22.4 per cent.

Much Remains To Be Done

Some unions continue to withhold membership from Negroes by provisions in their constitutions or by tradition. Others accept Negroes into "auxilliary" locals under the direction of a white parent union (a consistent practice until the 1960's in the AFL musicians unions). In some unions that accept Negro members, they may still be discriminated against either in job referrals, in upgrading, or in the exercise of seniority rights.

Other unions forbid any form of racial discrimination, and Negroes are welcomed and dealt with on the same basis as whites. For years the Brotherhood of Railway Trainmen maintained a "white only" provision in its constitution; however, in 1960, the Trainmen voted 4-1 to remove that stipulation. One fact is fairly evident: union racial attitudes are inconsistent; usually, but not always, they reflect local racial sentiments.

Two of the most exasperating problems facing Negroes have been the practice of "freezing" them in existing employment patterns when a plant is organized, and the refusal to place them as apprentices in some unions where special training is required, such as in the building trades. Discrimination in the building trades provoked a series of demonstrations at construction sites in several Northern cities early in the 1960's. During the summer of 1962, Negro and civil rights leaders asked New York City and Philadelphia officials to suspend projects where there were no Negro workers or where discrimination in hiring was most apparent. In some cases, after conferences with union leaders, more Negroes were

Worker on a construction project in the complicated network below the surface of New York City.
(Richard Saunders, Scope Associates)

Negro traffic policeman at intersection in suburban New York.
(Richard Saunders, Scope Associates)

hired, and a few have been brought into apprenticeship programs.

If changes in the Negro's status in so-called "blue collar"
occupations has been spasmodic, his advancement to white
collar positions has increased sharply in recent years. In 1965,
a number of major American corporations employed Negroes
in clerical or management positions, most of them for the first
time. Negro engineers and scientists are now playing important roles in research and development; Negro women are
employed as airline stewardesses, and a few Negro men are
now employed as airline pilots. Perhaps more important than
the present is what the future appears to promise. The fact
that major American enterprises are eagerly seeking qualified
Negroes from Negro businesses and from educational institutions across the land represents a major breakthrough for the
economic interests of American Negroes and for America.

Student traffic operator receiving initial training at the Michigan Bell
Telephone Company. In 1964, Secretary of Commerce Luther Hodges
established the Task Force for Equal Opportunity in Business.
(Michigan Bell Telephone)

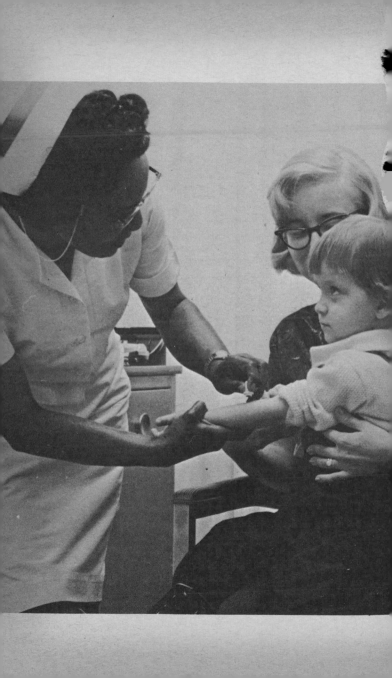

In 1960, Negroes comprised 17
per cent of the nursing profession.
(U.A.W. Solidarity)

File workers in the auto industry.
(*U.A.W. Solidarity*)

Two G.I.'s prepare an Easter basket for Der Führer.
(Department of the Army)

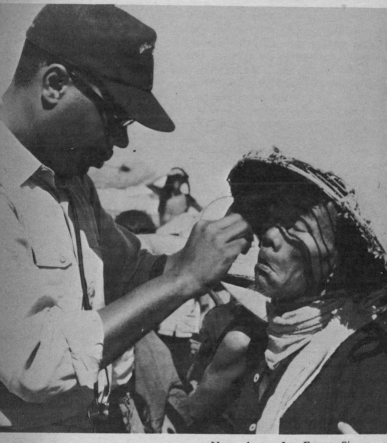

Navy doctor Lt. Ernest Simms applies medication to the infected eye of a South Vietnamese civilian. Dr. Simms accompanies Marines during surprise amphibious landings.
(Department of the Navy)

It would be very difficult to tell the whole story of the achievements of Negroes in government service in the United States, since Negro men and women have occupied a rather broad range of legislative, judicial, and executive positions at every level of government, in recent times especially. The Negro's chief experience in government has been, thus far, at the Federal level, but opportunities for political involvement at state and local levels are improving steadily. There are now fewer impediments to voting in the South, and because Negroes are moving into the cities of the North at an unprecedented rate, the Negro's participation in government, North and South, is steadily increasing. Many dedicated and competent Negroes are already serving in state and local governments across the land. We shall not attempt to list them here, except for one or two exceptional cases. Instead, we emphasize the Negro's participation in Federal service.

Government

The election of Franklin D. Roosevelt as President of the United States brought the New Deal to America; and with it, the so-called "Negro Brain Trust." Two of the first arrivals were Dr. Robert C. Weaver (who on January 17, 1966, became the first Negro cabinet member when he was appointed by President Johnson Secretary of the newly-created Department of Housing and Urban Development), and William H. Hastie (who is now a Judge of the United States Court of Appeals for the Third Circuit). Weaver and Hastie served in various Federal posts during the early New Deal days. By the 1940's, both men had become top-level Presidential advisors. The challenge of the New Deal also attracted Dr. James C. Evans, a distinguished graduate of Massachusetts Institute of Technology, from the faculty of West Virginia State College. After serving in several agencies, Dr. Evans became an official of the War Department in 1943. When the armed forces were unified in 1948, President Truman chose Evans to monitor the desegregation of the military establishment; and during the Eisenhower Administration, Dr. Evans directed the President's "People-To-People" program from an office in the Pentagon. He remained in Federal service as a senior Defense Department official under President John Kennedy.

In 1941, Ralph J. Bunche, a relatively unknown Howard University professor of political science, joined the staff of the Library of Congress. From 1942 to 1944, Dr. Bunche was chief research analyst in the supersecret Office of Strategic Services. Dr. Bunche became Under Secretary of the United Nations after distinguishing himself as a diplomat in the Arab-Israeli conflict of 1948. He shares with Dr. Martin Luther King, Jr., the honor of being one of the two Negro Americans to receive the Nobel Peace Prize.

Several Negroes have risen to prominence as American career diplomats. Clifton Wharton joined the State Department in 1924 as a Foreign Service Officer. He served in many responsible overseas and Washington posts before climaxing his career as United States Ambassador to Norway during the Kennedy Administration. Mr. Wharton spent thirty-nine years in the Foreign Service. The Norwegian Embassy was next headed by another Negro, Carl Rowan, who had been a naval officer in World War II. Mr. Rowan, a journalist by profession, served for a time as Director of the United States Information Agency in President Johnson's Administration, but resigned to devote his full time to writing. In 1966, six Negroes held the rank of Ambassador: Mercer Cook, Senegal; Patricia Harris, Luxembourg; Clinton Knox, Dahomey; James Nabrit, Jr., U. S. Mission to the United Nations; Hugh Smythe, Syria; Franklin Williams, Ghana; and Elliot Skinner, Upper Volta.

Negro civil servants have sometimes risen to unusual heights in the Federal service. One notable example is James Benton Parsons, who established a brilliant record as an Assistant United States Attorney for the Northern District of Illinois. Parsons left the Federal service in September, 1960, and was elected a Cook County (Chicago) Judge. Less than a year later, President Kennedy appointed him a United States District Judge in Chicago. This marked the first time a Negro had been appointed to the lifetime position of District Judge.

In very recent times, many Negroes have been members of Presidential official and unofficial families. J. Ernest Wilkins, a Chicago lawyer, was President Eisenhower's Assistant Secretary of Labor from 1953 to 1958. E. Frederick Morrow, a former executive of the Columbia Broadcasting System, served through President Eisenhower's second term as an Administrative Officer on the White House Staff. Andrew T. Hatcher, a California journalist, was President Kennedy's Associate Press Secretary. Louis Emanuel Martin, publisher of *The Michigan Chronicle* and former executive editor of *The Chicago Defender,* has served as chairman of the Democratic National Committee.

In June, 1967, President Johnson appointed Solicitor General Thurgood Marshall to the United States Supreme Court, making him the first Negro Justice of the highest court in the country. Justice Marshall, a native of Baltimore, was General Counsel of the NAACP before the late President Kennedy named him a judge of the U.S. Court of Appeals in 1961. In 1966, President Johnson appointed Mrs. Constance B. Motley, another NAACP lawyer, to be District Court Judge of the Southern District of New York.

Elsewhere in the Executive Branch Negroes serve in other responsible and difficult assignments. There are many Negro civil servants functioning at executive levels in such agencies as the Office of Economic Opportunity, the National Aeronautics and Space Administration, the Central Intelligence Agency, the Federal Aviation Agency, the National Security Agency, and the Agency for International Development.

To turn briefly from the exclusively Federal, there were, in 1967, eleven Negroes in the Georgia legislature, two in the Senate and nine in the House. This is a post-Reconstruction record for Negro representation in any state legislature. Also in 1967, Springfield, Ohio, a city of 82,000, elected a Negro mayor, and Carl B. Stokes and Richard G. Hatcher were elected the first black mayors of Cleveland and Gary respectively. Another Negro, Edward Brooke, former Attorney General for the state of Massachusetts, was elected to the United States Senate. He is the first Negro elected to sit in the United States Senate since 1874 during the waning years of the Reconstruction.

The Armed Forces

World War II opened many new doors for America's Negro citizens in the military services, although the doors had to be pushed open. In the early days of World War II, President Roosevelt's Secretary of War, Henry L. Stimson, was openly anti-Negro, for he believed that black Americans were unable to use the sophisticated equipment of modern warfare. An Army Air Force general told a group of Negro leaders at the beginning of World War II, "I don't know anyone who doesn't have blue eyes that can fly an airplane." Frank Knox, once the Secretary of the Navy, maintained that Negroes wouldn't stand and fight as combat sailors. Despite their courageous service in all the wars of this republic, such attitudes toward Negroes were very widely held. This is ironic, for just as it was Crispus Attucks, a runaway slave, who was first to give his life in the course of freedom in the American Revolution, so it was a Negro seaman, Dorie Miller, who, trained to serve white officers as a steward, seized an anti-aircraft gun from a dying white sailor and shot down four of the Japanese bombers that attacked Pearl Harbor on December 7, 1941. Admiral Chester Nimitz personally presented the Navy Cross to Miller on May 27, 1942.

Probably the most heartening news to reach Negro ears early in World War II was the announcement that black men would be trained as pilots for duty in the AAF. But that good news was tinged with overtones of prejudice, for it transpired that the Negro aviation cadets would be segregated at Tuskegee Army Air Field in Alabama. Strangely, the AAF trained non-flying officer candidates at an integrated school in

Miami, Florida (as did the Army Ground Forces and Army Service Forces at their installations).

The first class of Negro pilots was graduated on March 7, 1941 and consisted of only five men: Captain Benjamin O. Davis, Jr., a West Point graduate (his father, Brig. Gen. B. O. Davis, was commanding officer of the all-Negro 4th Cavalry); Lieutenants George Spencer Roberts; Mac Ross; Charles De-Bow, and Rodney Curtis. By April 1942, enough Negro pilots had been trained to activate the 99th Pursuit Squadron. Promoted to Major, Davis led the 99th in combat over North Africa against Field Marshal Rommel's famed Afrika Corps. As additional Negro pilots graduated from Tuskegee, the 99th was disbanded, and three new squadrons (the 100th, 301st, and 302nd Fighter Squadrons) were activated as the 332nd Fighter Group in October, 1942. Meantime, Davis had been promoted to full Colonel and became commanding officer of the 332nd.

The 332nd compiled one of the finest combat records of any AAF organization in World War II. The Group won acclaim for its performance escorting heavy bombers on some of the fiercest missions against the Axis powers.

As the war progressed, Negroes were trained as navigators, bombardiers, radio operators, gunners, and aerial engineers. Still, prejudice continued, especially against Negro AAF officers. With the activation of the all-Negro 477th Bomb Group (Medium), approximately 110 Negro flying officers were assigned for transition training in the B-25 bomber to Freeman Army Air Field near Seymour, Indiana. The 477th was commanded by a white officer, Colonel Robert R. Selway, Jr., who had assumed command in May 1943, at Selfridge Army Air Field near Detroit, Michigan. White officers were also receiving transition training at Freeman with the 477th. Colonel Selway decided that the white officers (many of whom had far fewer flying hours than the Negroes) were eligible to use the base's main officers' club; the Negro officers were directed to use a "student" officers' club of obviously inferior character. When the Negro officers tried to use the main club facility, more than a hundred of them were placed under arrest. General Ira Baker, Deputy Commander of the AAF, made a personal investigation of the case and made an immediate recommendation to the Pentagon. On January 15, 1945, the 477th got its own base at Godman Army Air Field near Louisville, Kentucky; and a new commanding officer—Colonel Benjamin O. Davis, Jr.

The most significant development in the creative arts is that Negroes are now appearing in roles that are not racially tied.
(Richard Saunders, Scope Associates)

The 477th was earmarked for duty on Okinawa in the Pacific, but the dropping of the atomic bomb in August 1945, brought the war to an end before the Group was dispatched overseas. Later, the 477th moved to Lockbourne Army Air Field near Columbus, Ohio. It remained an active AAF unit until the armed services were unified and desegregated in 1947.

Two all-Negro Infantry Divisions fought during World War II. In the European Theatre, the 92nd Infantry Division played a vital role in General Mark Clark's successful campaign in Italy. The heavy fighting cost the 92nd three thousand lives. Sixty-five Silver Stars, a hundred and sixty-two Bronze Stars, and thirteen hundred Purple Hearts went to the men of the 92nd. When the 1st and 29th Infantry Divisions landed in Normandy on June 6, 1944, the all-Negro 320th Barrage Balloon Battalion waded ashore with the first landing parties. The 320th was the only organization of its type in Europe; within hours of landing it had thrown up a protective cover of barrage balloons over the beachhead to prevent strafing attacks by German fighter planes.

Once the Allied armies broke through the hedgerows of Normandy, Lt. Gen. George S. Patton wheeled his mechanized Third U. S. Army straight for Paris and the Seine River. That was fine, except that Patton moved faster than anyone expected, and sustaining the Third Army became a major logistic problem. The superb performance of Negro Quartermaster truck drivers kept Patton supplied. Driving over unfamiliar roads and without headlights, the "Red Ball Express" became a U. S. Army legend.

Negro riflemen were part of the handful of Americans who fought the German counter-attack in the Battle of the Bulge during December 1944. And, in the Pacific, the 93rd Division fought its way across that ocean. The Division proved itself at Bougainville in the Solomon Islands, in the Dutch East Indies, Okinawa, and the Philippines.

The Korean War began with the American Negro soldier in the vanguard. With its history going back to the Civil War, the 24th Infantry Regiment was, in 1950, the oldest and only remaining all-Negro combat organization in the U. S. Army. As part of the 25th Division, the 24th Infantry had been on

Civil rights volunteer convasses in voter registration drive.
(Francis Mitchell, SNCC photo)

Negro Commissioned Officers and Enlisted Personnel

GRADES	USAF	Army	Navy	USMC	TOTALS
Generals and Admirals	1	0	0	0	
Colonels and Captains	6	6	0	0	
Lt. Cols. and Commanders	67	117	3	0	
Majors and Lieut. Commanders	124	424	17	0	
Captains and Lieutenants	615	1,532	88	7	
1st Lieuts. and Lieuts. (j.g.)	317	650	57	16	
2nd Lieuts. and Ensigns	170	421	29	9	
Totals	1,300	3,150	174	32	4,656
E-9	32	76	22	5	
E-8	140	586	89	19	
E-7	616	3,143	984	142	
E-6	2,115	10,496	2,843	417	
E-5	10,287	21,892	5,370	1,490	
E-4	14,321	21,133	6,771	2,663	
E-3	11,505	26,385	7,502	3,101	
E-2	6,951	10,836	5,396	3,727	
E-1	597	8,456	1,431	1,787	
Totals	26,564	103,210	30,418	13,351	173,543

duty in Japan when hostilities commenced. Rushed to Korea, the 24th gave the United Nations its first victory over the Communist invaders when it routed them from Yechon on July 20, 1950. A Negro officer, 2nd Lieutenant William Benefield, Jr., became one of the nation's first Korean War heroes, earning a posthumous Distinguished Service Cross while clearing a mine field during the July campaign.

As part of a fully integrated United States Air Force, Negro pilots and crewmen added new laurels to the nation's youngest military service; several Negroes earned Distinguished Flying Crosses. One of the most outstanding participants in the Asian crisis was Brigadier General Benjamin O. Davis, Jr., in command of Task Force 13, the USAF defense organization for the island of Formosa. As a Major General, Davis was Deputy Chief of Staff for Operations, United States Air Force, Europe, until 1961. He then served as Director of Manpower and Organization. Later, he was named Deputy Commander of United States Forces in Korea.

In the Vietnamese War, from fifteen to thirty-four per cent of the combat troops have been Negroes, although Negroes constitute only eleven per cent of the American population. A good percentage of the Negro troops are "first line," while Negroes are disproportionately represented in extra-hazardous or elite fighting units like the paratroopers, for which they volunteer. They serve in completely integrated units, and their officers invariably rate them as excellent fighting men.

Not until October 30, 1954, by order of the Defense Department, was the long-standing policy of all-Negro units in the armed forces completely abolished. It had taken over ninety years and many Negro lives given in defense of their country before the Negro soldier was permitted to fight and die, if need be, by the side of his white counterpart. Now, thoughout the American armed services, Negroes are serving in every type of assignment. Negro aircraft commanders with racially-mixed crews are at the controls of multi-jet bombers of the Strategic Air Command. A Negro Army officer is Director of Intelligence for an entire Army area in the United States. And a Negro naval officer commands one of our fastest destroyers in the Pacific Ocean.

June 1963 Report of the President's Committee on Equal Opportunity in the Armed Forces. 1962 data for all Services. The Air Force figures include only officers assigned to duty in the 48 States of the Continental United States. All other figures are complete and worldwide in scope.

Business

The Negro businessman has suffered from five persistent difficulties which have seriously limited his chance to compete realistically as an entrepreneur: (1) insufficient capital and credit; (2) inadequate training and experience; (3) lack of choice operating locations; (4) a racially-restricted patronage; and (5) the inability to organize for cooperative effort. The first four difficulties are directly traceable to racial discrimination; the fifth is largely a psychological factor which may be indirectly related to the existence of racial bias. Because Negroes have such a moderate history of success in business, and because Negroes constitute an economically deprived class with little money for investment, plus the psychological factor [lack of self-confidence], the Negro businessman has not been able to organize large-scale public subscription of shares, the backbone of the American corporation.

Until some time after the Civil War, Negro business in the North and South was restricted to small, family-held service establishments, like restaurants, cleaning shops, etc. The final twelve years of the nineteenth century saw a slight change in the pattern as Negro banks were organized in several Southern states. The first Negro bank was the Savings Bank of the Grand Fountain Order of True Reformers, in Richmond, Virginia. There followed in rapid succession four other Negro banks: the Mutual Trust Co. of Chattanooga (1889); the Alabama Penny Savings Bank of Birmingham (1890); the Nickel Savings Bank of Richmond, Virginia (1896); and the St. Luke's Savings Bank, also of Richmond.

Negro banking grew rapidly during the early part of this century. Between 1888 and 1934, 134 Negro-controlled banks were established, mostly in the South and in three Northern states. The resources of Negro banks reached a high point in 1929, with thirty institutions holding nearly thirteen million dollars in deposits. The bank failures of the Depression era wiped out most of the Negro bankers. By 1931, their total resources had dropped to seven million dollars.

Insurance

The life insurance field has been the most rewarding one, financially, that American Negroes have entered. Before the Civil War, countless beneficial and mutual aid societies flourished among free Negroes. The Grand United Order of True Reformers pioneered by offering insurance protection to its members. Other lodges such as the Masons, Odd Fellows, and Knights of Pythias adopted the same plan. The early beneficial associations provided the training and the experience that Negroes needed in the business of risk. Most of the companies were short-lived, but a few developed into substantial insurance operations.

The first Negro legal reserve life insurance company was founded by a Negro physician who believed that the fraternal companies could not survive. Dr. William A. Attaway organized the Mississippi Life Insurance Company in 1909, with 50,000 dollars of borrowed capital. By 1922, the company had expanded its operations into Arkansas, Tennessee, and Texas, and had a premium income of 881,668 dollars with fifteen million dollars of insurance in force. The Mississippi Life later merged with the Standard Life Insurance Company of Atlanta, headed by Herman Perry. Perry had gained broad experience in life insurance while working as an agent for white companies. Although he organized Standard Life four years after Mississippi Life was founded, Perry had caught up with and passed the older firm by 1922. At the time of the merger Standard Life had 1,200,000 dollars of premium income supporting twenty-three million dollars of insurance in force.

The most dramatic growth of a Negro insurance company has been that of the North Carolina Mutual Life Insurance Company. Based in Durham, North Carolina, the firm began operations in 1900. Dr. A. M. Moore and John Merrick, a barber, laid down a basic principle: North Carolina Mutual was to emphasize the business aspects of insurance as opposed to fraternal considerations. Dr. Moore remained mostly in the background while Merrick and William J. Kennedy sparked the company. Neither Merrick nor Kennedy was a formally educated man, but they were both highly intelligent businessmen. When the company faced its first death claim, there was only twenty-nine cents in cash on hand. Merrick and Kennedy dug into their own pockets for the ten-dollar payment. The widow who received the payment gladly signed a receipt, and that document became North Carolina Mutual's best advertisement.

North Carolina Mutual holds the distinction of having produced the country's first professionally trained actuary, Asa T. Spaulding. The cousin of a prominent Negro attorney, Asa Spaulding earned a *magna cum laude* degree in mathematics from New York University before completing actuarial science studies at the University of Michigan. William J. Kennedy became President of the company in 1958, but relinquished the presidency to Spaulding the next year.

Today, North Carolina Mutual ranks high among the nation's more than 1,500 life insurance companies. Its operations reach into fourteen states in the North and South, with 345 million dollars of insurance in force. A new twelve-story building in the heart of Durham houses the firm's home office. This building is the city's highest structure and the nation's largest office building owned by Negroes.

The Creative Arts

To chronicle Negro attainments in America's creative and artistic life is a large undertaking; the area is broad and the contributions of Negroes many. Moreover, an apology should preface such an attempt, because citing some Negroes who have become famous tends to minimize the achievement of others. Nevertheless, the successful Negro in the creative arts expresses the emotional spirit of his race, for much of the art of the American Negro derives from and reflects the precariousness of his position in American society. If protest is the bedrock of all artistic endeavor, it is all the more so in respect to the art of the American Negro.

During the height of the slavocracy and those terrible years following the Civil War, American Negro creativity was geared to the plantations and reflected the lowly status of the Negro as a slave, or as a newly freed ex-slave. In a remarkable book called *The Souls of Black Folk*, W. E. B. DuBois crystallized a growing opposition to the accommodationist philosophies of Booker T. Washington which, however inadvertently, had served to keep the Negro, his spirit, and his art earthbound.

Greenville, Mississippi, Freedom
School, part of the Summer 1964
Project to promote voter registra-
tion.
(Cliff Vaughs, SNCC photo)

DuBois' collection of essays, when they were published in 1903, signaled the beginning of a new era in Negro art, and a new concept of the Negro's self-respect. His interpretation of the Negro's "double consciousness" which derived from his being technically free but restrained and inhibited in every conceivable way, broke the psychological dependence upon the slavery experience which had so limited Negro art and self-expression.

Two outstanding American Negro poets at the turn of this century were Paul Laurence Dunbar and James Weldon Johnson. While a high school student, Dunbar decided he wanted to be a poet. Although he was required to take menial jobs after completing school, his passion to write never subsided. After paying to have two volumes of his work published, Dunbar found an effective patron in William Dean Howells, a noted novelist, essayist, and editor. Howells helped Dunbar secure a publisher and provided the guidance that eventually saw the Dayton, Ohio, Negro establish himself, both in this country and in Europe, as a distinguished writer. As for Johnson, his *Lif' Ev'ry Voice and Sing* progressed from a vehicle of Negro hope to an American musical classic. Johnson's *Fifty Years and Other Poems,* published in 1917, was a literary bridge between the Great Negro Migration of the early twentieth century and the birth of what has been termed the Negro Renaissance.

Following World War I, New York's Harlem and Chicago's South Side were, to many Negro artists, what Paris was to their white colleagues. The spotlight of public recognition shifted from the Negroes of letters to black Americans in the performing arts. Like their white counterparts, these performers often had to work in prohibition-era dives where the cigarette smoke blurred the audience's vision, while bootleg whisky dulled their senses. The jazz of Louis Armstrong, Duke Ellington, Bessie Smith, Jimmie Lunceford, and Noble Sissle came to prominence · during the "Roaring Twenties," the era of the underworld gangsters who fought for control of our large cities.

President Roosevelt's New Deal and the Federal Theatre and Writers' projects were instrumental in the advancement of Negro creative effort during the Depression years. A partial list of artists and writers who benefited from the program includes Langston Hughes, Gwendolyn Brooks, Melvin Tolson, Richard Durham, Robert Hayden, Owen Dodson, Myron O'Higgins, M. Carl Holman, and Vertis Hayes. The Depression years also saw the launching of such Negro writers as Zora Neal Hurston, George Henderson, Waters Turpin, William Attaway, and Arna Bontemps. The Forties brought recognition to Richard Wright, Ralph Ellison, Frank Yerby, Ann Petry, and Rei Ottley. During the past fifteen years, another procession of Negro American writers has been added to our literature, including Lorraine Hansberry, James Baldwin, John O. Killens, and LeRoi Jones.

America's music has been enriched by the contributions of Paul Robeson, William Dawson, Dean Dixon, Mahalia Jackson, Billie Holiday, Ella Fitzgerald, and Harry Belafonte, as well as Todd Duncan, William Warfield, George Shirley, Dorothy Mayner, Roland Hayes, and Ann Brown. Marian Anderson was the first American Negro to sing at New York City's Metropolitan Opera, which has since added Leontyne Price, Mattiwilda Dobbs, Grace Bumbry, and Robert McFerrin to its company.

The Negro has also recently been granted recognition in the fields of commercial and illustrative art. Outstanding examples include advertising executive George Olden and *Life* magazine photographer Gordon Parks. In the fine arts, Negro painters and sculptors have made notable contributions: Hale Woodruff, Jacob Lawrence, Elizabeth Prophet, Sargent Johnson, Vertis Hayes, William Scott, Horace Pippin, Augusta Savage, and Selma Burke.

For years, Broadway and Hollywood shackled Negro casting to the stereotype established by D. W. Griffith in his pro-Ku Klux Klan film, *The Birth of a Nation*. During the thirties and early forties, Negro movie audiences were often embarrassed by the blatantly "Uncle Tom" roles handed to such performers as Bill Robinson, Rochester, Fredi Washington, and Louise Beavers. Gradually, the roles of Negro performers began to reflect the changing position of the Negro in American society. Competition from other media has helped create new roles for Negroes both in films and on the stage. Such performers as Hilda Sims, Diana Sands, Diahann Carroll, Ossie Davis, Ruby Dee, Sammy Davis, Jr., and Academy Award-winner Sidney Poitier are now well known to most Americans. Nor is the Negro any longer limited exclusively and automatically by the color of his skin. It is not uncommon for a Negro nowadays to be cast without attention to his pigment; as, in fact, a human being.

The Executive branch of the government ended slavery with the Emancipation Proclamation, the Legislative branch passed the Fourteenth Amendment declaring the Negro a citizen; but the Judicial branch evaded the earlier actions. In *Scott v. Sanford* (1857), the Court held that a Negro had no rights a white man was required to respect. Thirty-nine years later, the Court's decision in *Plessy v. Ferguson,* established the doctrine of separate but equal facilities for Negroes and whites. These two monumental rulings from the nation's highest tribunal forebode second-class citizenship for the Negro American. However, in recent years, the Supreme Court has become the institution most reflective of the pervading spirit of American democracy, and less reflective of the passing "mood of the times." This change is most dramatically illustrated in the areas of voting rights, interstate travel, and schooling.

Voting Rights

For years, Negroes were effectively disenfranchised by the so-called "white primary." By excluding Negroes from voting in its primary elections, Southern Democrats nullified any vote a Negro might cast in the General Election. Negroes were also excluded from participation in the conventions, caucuses, and mass meetings of the party; and, of course, they could not run for office. The white primary fell before the Court's 1944 decision in *Smith v. Allwright*. The decision declared that the primary election was an integral part of the governmental election machinery, and that it was unconstitutional for it to be operated on a racial basis. Even with the decision in *Smith v. Allwright*, the Negro's right to an effective exercise of the ballot has not been cleared. The remaining problem has been formidable: how to overcome the many barriers that keep Negroes off the voting lists altogether. Until 1957, the Department of Justice could not legally protect the right to vote. The Civil Rights Acts of 1957 and 1960 have given the Department such authority, and with the passing of the Voting Rights Act of 1965 (the provisions of which have been upheld by the Supreme Court), the Federal government has the unquestionable legal means to enforce and protect the voting rights of all American citizens in states, territories, or other political subdivisions which have discriminatory voting regulations.

Signed by President Johnson on August 6, 1965, the Voting Rights Act: (1) Suspends literacy tests and other devices, found to be discriminatory, as qualifications for voting in the states of Alabama, Alaska, Georgia, Louisiana, Mississippi, South Carolina, Virginia, and at least twenty-six counties in North Carolina; (2) Provides for the assignment of Federal examiners to see that registration is conducted on an open basis and, if need be, to conduct the registration themselves; (3) Directs the U. S. Attorney General to bring suits immediately to test the constitutionality of poll taxes which abridge the right to vote; and (4) Extends protection under civil and criminal law to qualified persons seeking to vote and to those who urge or aid others to vote. Some of the areas covered by the Act do not have records of voting rights discrimination, but do have laws on their books which could be used for this purpose. The real struggle, and the area at which the bill is directed, is in the hard-core Southern states that have consistently prevented Negroes from voting.

Signs from Southern waiting rooms are on their way out.
(Ed Bagwell, NAACP)

The fight for equal voting rights has not yet been won. Actually, the Voting Rights Act sets the groundwork for a hard and long fight. The fact that there are laws on the books protecting the Negro's right to vote does not mean that there will no longer be attempts to prevent him from using it. The Negro still faces intimidation and the possible failure of careful enforcement of the laws. While there is no question that a major victory has been won with the passing of the 1965 Voting Rights Act, only the future will reveal the success or failure of America to fulfill its commitment.

On orders of Governor Orval Faubus, National Guardsmen turn back four of the nine Negro students who tried to enter all-white Central High School in Little Rock, Arkansas, in 1957. *(Wide World Photos)*

Interstate Travel

With better mass transportation, America has become increasingly mobile, and accommodations for the traveler have become matters of public necessity. A seat on a train or bus, rest facilities in bus and train stations and airports, and facilities in motels and hotels, have become as important as owning an automobile or house. White Americans take for granted the availability of such accommodations; but for years they were frequently unavailable to Negro travelers.

Traditionally, railways, bus stations, and airport facilities all over the South were segregated. Negroes traveling North were required to sit in segregated railway coaches until the trains crossed the historical division between North and South, the Mason-Dixon line. Traveling South, Negroes, on crossing the line, had to leave their seats in the more comfortable coaches they had shared with white riders and transfer to older, less comfortable coaches. Pullman accommodation was not available to Negroes in most Southern cities, as this would have required their traveling in intimate proximity with white passengers. Similar restrictions operated against Negroes in the use of buses traveling within and between Southern states.

In 1944, a Negro passenger refused to give up her seat and move to the rear of a bus operated by the Virginia Greyhound Lines; she was convicted of violating Virginia's segregation laws. The Supreme Court reversed the conviction in *Morgan v. Virginia,* citing the need for uniformity in the regulation of interstate commerce. Since at least eighteen states forbade segregation and at least ten required it, it seemed an unreasonable and unnecessary burden on the passengers and the carriers to require compliance with differing local segregation laws as public vehicles moved from state to state. Six years later, in *Henderson v. United States,* the Court struck down an Interstate Commerce Commission (ICC) ruling requiring Negro passengers in railroad dining cars to eat behind a curtain separating them from other passengers in the diner. Various devices were employed by both the railroads and buses in attempts to subvert both the Morgan and

Pickets rest under police guard during 1963 demonstrations against Jim Crow trade unions in New York City.
(Cecil Layne, NAACP)

Henderson decisions. In 1955, the ICC also ordered the end of segregated facilities in bus and train terminal buildings.

Desegregation of the Universities

Free public education is one of the fundamental rights of the American citizen. But for several reasons, Negroes have not shared fully in this right. Lack of economic means has, historically, been the impediment to a well-educated Negro minority. And apathy—caused by the feeling that education is useless because it does not lead to commensurate employment —has stifled the normal incentive of tens of thousands of Negro boys and girls. Resentment, too, has taken its toll, consuming energies that might have gone into learning and creative expression.

There have been other reasons for the Negro's lag in education, not the least of which has been the dearth and poor quality of public school facilities available to non-whites. From 1896 until 1954, the "separate but equal" doctrine enunciated in *Plessy v. Ferguson* was the philosophy regulating educational facilities for Negroes throughout the South and in many of the border states as well.

Four important opportunities to repudiate the Plessy doctrine came before the courts in the two decades leading up to the historic desegregation cases of 1954. In these four cases, the courts kept within the doctrine, but gradually whittled away its original meaning. In the first of these cases (argued in 1935), Donald Murray, a Negro graduate of Amherst College, was denied admission to the University of Maryland Law School solely because of his race. The University offered, instead, to pay Murray's tuition at any other law school that would accept him. The Maryland Court of Appeals found the requirement that he leave the state and forego the advantages inherent in studying law in Maryland, where he planned to practice, to be *de facto* inequality under the Plessy rule. "Equal treatment can be furnished only in the existing (University of Maryland) Law School," the court held, and ordered Murray admitted forthwith.

In 1938, Lloyd Gaines, a Negro who had been denied admission to the University of Missouri Law School, was ordered admitted because the state of Missouri did not provide separate but equal law schools for Negroes. Gaines did not reap the fruits of his Supreme Court victory, for he mysteriously disappeared very soon after the decision was handed down. His fate has never been determined.

Forewarned by the decisions in the Maryland and Missouri cases, several Southern states moved hastily to set up segregated law schools for Negroes. None of them was equal to the white schools maintained by the states in terms of physical plant, libraries, or teaching faculties. So Negroes continued to sue for admission to the better schools.

In a 1950 suit involving the University of Texas Law School (*Sweat v. Painter*), the complainant, supported by briefs submitted by the United States government, contended that the separate but equal doctrine laid down fifty-four years earlier in *Plessy v. Ferguson* should be disavowed. The defendants, backed by pro-segregation arguments presented by the attorneys-general of eleven Southern states, urged the U. S. Supreme Court to endorse the Plessy doctrine and to make it specifically applicable to all areas of public education.

The Court refused to adopt either of the positions urged upon it, but it did rule that the state-supported, segregated law school for Negroes was not equal to the "white" University of Texas school. Its decision involved an important extension of the concept of equality, for the Court held that the University of Texas Law School possessed certain intangible qualities, lacking in the segregated institution, that make for greatness in a law school. It was becoming increasingly clear that equality could not be limited to bricks and mortar, or even to an equal number of teachers with commensurate degrees and experience. Equality involved the uninhibited interactions both of people with people and with institutions. It meant the opportunity for the normal range of social and intellectual experiences that are possible only in an open society. The Court had thus moved closer to the inevitable conclusion that equality cannot abide the forced separation of human beings on the basis of the color of their skins.

In *McLaurin v. Board of Regents,* decided the same day as the Sweat case, the Supreme Court took yet another step toward restoring to the Negro his civil rights and his human dignity. The Court now ruled that a Negro student who had been admitted to the Graduate School of the University of Oklahoma could not be required to eat, study, or attend classes under segregated conditions. McLaurin had been assigned a "colored" seat in each classroom, and had been further humiliated by being required to eat in a designated corner of the school cafeteria. A segregated table had been set aside for him in the library. The Court ruled that while individuals were free to avoid association with McLaurin, the state could not impose restrictions "which prohibit the intellectual commingling of students. . . ."

The Plessy doctrine still stood, but it was no longer intact. Little by little, its once-broad applications were being eroded. On an historic Monday in May 1954, the separate but equal doctrine of *Plessy v. Ferguson* would be destroyed forever.

Desegregation of the Schools

In failing to repudiate the separate but equal doctrine in the law school cases, the Court quite properly observed the long-established practice of refusing to rule on questions not directly relevant to the case under adjudication. The issues in the law school cases were solely a matter of whether the separate provisions for the education of Negroes were, in fact, equal to those for whites. The question of whether anything "separate" could, by definition, also be "equal," was not then in litigation. In the early 1950's, however, the Court was faced with precisely this question in a series of suits seeking to enable Negro children to attend public schools then closed to them on racial grounds. The supreme tribunal was now called upon either to broaden unequivocally the separate but equal doctrine of Plessy, or to extend the liberalizing principles of the Sweat and McLaurin cases to their logical extremes: either to find segregated primary and secondary schools to be constitutional, or to find all segregated schools to be unconstitutional. This was the significance of the case of *Brown v. Board of Education*, decided on May 17, 1954. In its decision, the Court first noted that "education is perhaps the most important function of the state. . . . It is the very foundation of good citizenship . . . [and] a principal instrument in awakening the child to cultural values, in preparing him for later professional training, and in helping him adjust normally to his environment. . . . The opportunity of an education . . . [which] the state has undertaken to provide . . . is a right which must be made available to all on equal terms."

The Court then defined the issues before it: "Does segregation of children in public schools solely on the basis of race, even though the physical facilities and other tangible factors may be equal, deprive the children of the minority group of equal educational opportunities?" Said the Court, "We believe that it does."

The unanimous decision was a final and certain requiem for *Plessy v. Ferguson.* "Separate educational facilities are inherently unequal," the Court ruled; and "in the field of public education the doctrine of 'separate but equal' has no place."

The Principle Extended

The decision of the Supreme Court in *Brown v. Board of Education* rests, primarily, upon the equal protection clause of the Fourteenth Amendment to the Constitution, which guarantees to all citizens equal protection under the law. In the companion case of *Bolling v. Sharpe,* involving segregation in the public schools of the District of Columbia, the Court broadened its constitutional base to include the due process clause of the Fifth Amendment, holding that "racial discrimination . . . is a denial of the due process of law." It is upon these two constitutional provisions that much of the civil rights litigation of recent years has been based.

The five suits comprising the *Brown v. Board of Education* are so-called "class actions," for they affect not only the rights of the original plaintiffs, but also those of all other Americans, of whatever race, who are similarly concerned. The Brown case was specifically directed at segregation in public elementary and high schools; its principle was extended to the field of higher education in 1956 in the case of *Florida, ex rel. Hawkins v. Board of Control,* in which the Supreme Court ordered Virgil Hawkins, a forty-eight year old Negro, admitted to the College of Law of the University of Florida without delay. Within two years of the Brown case, the principle of the "inherent" inequality of racially segregated facilities had been extended to parks and playgrounds, housing, transportation, and many other aspects of American life in which segregation had been traditional. Monday, May 17, 1954, was an auspicious day for the future of American democracy. It was the day America cleared its conscience and began the long road back to the shrine of its founding principles.

The South Reacts

Within a few weeks of the historic decision in *Brown v. Board of Education,* the first White Citizens Council was organized in Mississippi. Allied units and independent Councils were soon organized in every Southern state, and a massive campaign to oppose the implementation of the Court's ruling was soon underway.

The primary targets of the White Citizens Councils have been individual Negroes who advocate desegregation or who participate in petitions, law suits, or other activities aimed at the elimination of segregation. White liberals have also found themselves the objects of vituperation. The principle weapon used to discourage desegregation has been economic reprisal. Negroes suspected of membership in the NAACP have, in some areas, been fired from their jobs if they were employed by whites. Whites who supported desegregation or who refused to fire Negro employees when ordered to do so by the Councils have had their businesses boycotted, and their families harassed and intimidated.

In some areas, in Mississippi particularly, Negroes have been murdered in mysterious circumstances, and others have been beaten by unknown assailants. Many Negro churches and homes have been bombed and burned. The Councils disclaim responsibility for any violence Negro integrationists have suffered, but their common identification with the Ku Klux Klan and the frequency of overlapping memberships with the Klan make such disavowals questionable.

In those areas in which the Councils' strength is greatest, they have created an atmosphere of fear and intimidation sufficient to frighten some Negroes and to silence many respectable white people. But even in Mississippi, where their Gestapo-like influence is greatest, the Councils have been unable to frighten or silence *all* the people. Negroes still insist upon enjoying the full privileges of citizenship, and they are still supported in their efforts by significant numbers of whites. Indeed, the influence of the White Citizens Councils has dropped sharply except for Mississippi, and although they still

National Guardsmen dragging SNCC photographer, Cliff Vaughs.
(Danny Lyon, SNCC photo)

have some power in Alabama and Louisiana, more moderate elements are in control elsewhere in the South.

One of the more frightening aspects of the reaction of white Southerners to the drive for civil rights has been the increase in the power of the Ku Klux Klans. There is no longer one unified Klan. There are, rather, a number of Klans, each having similar objectives but different leadership and control of different geographical areas. While it is true that in a few areas of the South more moderate elements have reduced the power of the Klans, it is still all too common that, as the White Citizens Councils lose power, the Klans move in and find ready acceptance or complete apathy on the part of the responsible white community. The Klans have become the symbol and the instrument of last-ditch resistance to change.

Desegregation: Peaceful And Violent

When the decision in the Brown case was announced on May 17, 1954, the governors of some states, Delaware, Tennessee, North Carolina, Kentucky, Maryland, and Oklahoma among them, issued public statements announcing their expectations that the Supreme Court's interpretation of the law would be respected and the Court's requirements put into operation.

In the Deep South, however, the Court's ruling was denounced by most governors. Governor Talmadge of Georgia declared that integration would never take place in his state. The governor of Mississippi hastily summoned a hundred Negro leaders to a conference at which he offered them a plan for "voluntary segregation." When the Negroes issued a statement declaring themselves "unalterably opposed to any effort . . . to attempt to circumvent the decision of the Supreme Court . . . ," the governor described himself as "stunned" that the Negroes of his state would adopt such an attitude.

In the fall of 1954, four large cities—Washington, D. C., Wilmington, St. Louis, and Baltimore—began to desegregate their public schools. At least forty smaller towns and cities followed suit. Within a year, more than half the counties of West Virginia had desegregated some or all of their schools. In Arizona and Kansas, segregated schools were virtually eliminated. In Pasadena, California, and in more than a hundred school districts in Missouri, the schools were quickly integrated. Negroes were not the only beneficiaries of this trend, for New York State's practice of segregating Indian school children was finally discontinued.

Nowhere did the efforts to resist integration succeed. Just as the schools of Delaware were integrated, so were the schools at Clinton, Sturgis, Nashville, Little Rock, and New Orleans integrated, despite racist agitators. In the capital city of Georgia, where Governor Griffin had promised that no integration would take place, desegregation did, in fact, come with little more than a ripple in the everyday life of the Atlanta metropolis. In the big cities of Dallas, Memphis, Houston, integration came quietly after the troublemakers were warned they would go to jail. Eight years after the Brown decision, desegregation had taken place in 948 school districts; in only a handful had there been any significant resistance.

Little Rock

The American Negro often complains that he is judged by the worst behavior of the least responsible members of his group—and that his judges do not consider all the facts. Similarly, Little Rock, Arkansas, has been unfairly represented internationally. It is not generally known outside the South that, prior to the unfortunate events surrounding the desegregation of Central High School in the autumn of 1957, Little Rock was considered a liberal town by most Southern Negroes and whites. Evidence supports that point of view. In the first place, despite its relatively low standard of living, the state of Arkansas had taken a notable lead among its sister states in the South abandoning the traditional practice of total segregation. As early as 1948, Arkansas had voluntarily admitted Negroes to the graduate division of the state university, the first Southern state to do so of its own accord. In 1954, the public schools at Fayetteville and Charleston were desegregated, as were Roman Catholic schools at Fort Smith and Paris. A year later, the public schools at Hoxie and all state-supported undergraduate colleges discarded segregation. There were no incidents.

By 1955, Negroes in Arkansas had made significant gains

Civil Rights marchers outside the White House, demonstrating their agreement with Southern sit-ins. (On pages 138–139)
(Martin Miller)

in employment areas usually reserved in the South for whites. There were Negro guards at the Pine Bluff Arsenal; business firms throughout the state had begun to hire Negro salesmen; the hospitals in the larger cities employed both white and Negro nurses. Some Scout troops and Scout camp facilities were integrated; some county medical societies and labor unions had quietly dispensed with Jim Crow practices. The American Association of University Women accepted Negro members. By the same token, the Arkansas Council on Human Relations had published a manual on desegregation for the use of school districts soon to be involved in this new way of living and learning together.

In the city of Little Rock itself, Negroes and whites had long enjoyed amicable relations. Integrated meetings and conferences were frequently held in the best hotels in the city, and although Negroes were not yet accepted as overnight guests, it seemed likely that such restrictions were soon to be dropped. Full library services were available to all Little Rock citizens, irrespective of race, and Negroes attended the city-sponsored symphony concerts and other cultural events without inconvenience of any kind.

By 1957, the Little Rock School Board was ready to begin the voluntary program of gradual desegregation on which it had been working since 1954. The plan envisaged desegregation of senior high school grades in September 1957, with desegregation of the lower grades to be completed within six years. In February 1957, the Arkansas Legislature passed four segregation bills designed to circumvent desegregation. These bills were all signed by Governor Orville Faubus. However, in dramatic public support of the school board's plans, the citizens of Little Rock went to the polls in March and, by decisive majorities, elected to the school board two men who were publicly committed to the desegregation plan. Little Rock thus announced to the world that it was ready to comply with the law of the land.

What happened subsequently is an unfortunate and inaccurate reflection on a majority of the people of Little Rock and Arkansas. Blame for the trouble that followed in Little Rock and in other cities of the South must probably rest, in part, upon seventy-seven United States Representatives and nineteen Senators from the South, who issued the unfortunate 1956 "Southern Manifesto" denouncing the Supreme Court's school decisions of 1954. The so-called manifesto did much to encourage dissident elements in the several states of the

South to question the legality of the Court's ruling and to defy its desegregation orders.

Another event contributing to the defiance of the segregationists in Little Rock was the appearance in that city of Georgia's Governor Marvin Griffin. Griffin, a rabid segregationist, went to Little Rock to address a White Citizens Council rally in late August, just one week before desegregation was scheduled to take place at Central High School. Governor Faubus, who was considered a "moderate" by both whites and Negroes, telephoned Governor Griffin two days before his scheduled appearance and requested that he not come to Little Rock if his address were likely to increase racial tensions.

Despite his assurances to Governor Faubus, Griffin delivered an inflammatory speech that perceptibly increased the feeling against desegregation in Little Rock. At what point the Governor of Arkansas stopped being a "moderate" and became a segregationist is difficult to determine, but Governor Faubus evidently made this transition. His behavior in calling out the National Guard to turn away Negro students from Central High School saddened America and shocked the world.

Little Rock thus became a symbol of the "frictions and abrasions" of social change. But Little Rock is not the true face of America; nor is New Orleans or Oxford, Mississippi, or Birmingham or Selma, Alabama. These cities-in-turmoil represent one aspect of life in America as America attempts to work out its problems of readjustment between races. America's efforts to make the democratic values of its society meaningful to all the people are frequently tardy and sometimes lacking in dynamism. But the efforts have been made, and they have been approved by most of the people. However difficult social adjustment may be, the democratic process must prevail. It did prevail in Little Rock, and it will in all similar cases.

The Rise of Civil Rights Groups

Mrs. Rosa Parks was comfortable in the bus seat she occupied on December 1, 1955. Her refusal to move to a segregated seat in the back of the vehicle signaled one of the most successful campaigns for dignity Negroes have ever waged in the South. It also brought into existence the Montgomery Improvement Association, headed by Dr. Martin Luther King, Jr. With Dr. King and Rev. Ralph Abernathy providing leadership, the Negroes of Montgomery, Alabama, mounted a hundred per cent effective boycott against Montgomery's Jim Crow city bus system. The Negroes demanded two acts by the city: an end to segregated seating on buses, and the employment of Negro drivers on routes moving through Negro neighborhoods. The economic effect of the boycott brought the bus company to the conference table in an attempt to reach a settlement. Negotiations soon broke off, and the Negroes took their cause to court. A Federal district court ruled on June 5, 1956, that segregation on local public transportation violated both the "due process" and the "equal protection of the law" provisions of the Fourteenth Amendment. Almost a year after Mrs. Parks' arrest in the original incident, the U. S. Supreme Court upheld the lower court's decision. In December 1956, Montgomery, Alabama, desegregated its entire public transportation system.

The Montgomery boycott demonstrated the power of organized effort by Negroes in Southern communities. Early in 1957, Dr. King and other church leaders formed the Southern Christian Leadership Conference. The hallmark of SCLC activity is non-violence, and Dr. King's steadfast devotion to that principle has lifted him to international prominence. In 1964, he became the second Negro American to be awarded the Nobel Peace Prize.

The struggle for Negro rights has taken many forms and has involved at least four major organizations in addition to SCLC. The NAACP (National Council for the Advancement of Colored People) has been in the forefront of legal battles for civil rights for more than half a century. Today, it has grown to an organization of nearly 500,000 members in the fifty states of the Union. Its board of directors and national staff are interracial; NAACP presidents have been white traditionally, while the executive secretaries or executive directors have always been Negroes. Its Legal Defense and Educational Fund, long headed by Thurgood Marshall, established an impressive record of success in civil rights cases with approximately eleven victories for each loss in the United States Supreme Court.

Although it is known primarily for its legal activity in prosecuting civil rights cases, the NAACP also sponsors several programs designed to educate the public concerning race relations. It also supports and opposes legislation affecting the

Sit-in demonstration in New Mexico to protest brutality and discrimination against Negroes, especially in housing.
(CORE)

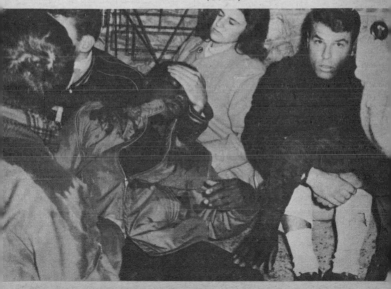

Malcolm X, one of the most charismatic Negro leaders of the century.
(Richard Saunders, Pictorial Parade)

civil rights movement, and defends direct action, such as protest demonstrations. The Association's educational program
seeks to create positive settings for legal and social change by
preparing both whites and Negroes in specific communities
to accept such changes with a minimum of conflict. Whites
are urged to comply with the law, and Negroes are trained to
utilize existing rights of citizenship in such areas as voting,
Federal employment, and education. Under the guidance of
the late Walter White, its first Executive Secretary and, more
recently, Executive Director Roy Wilkins, the NAACP has
grown in influence, membership, and public acceptance.

Second to appear on the scene was the National Urban
League, which has pioneered in helping the Negro make the
transition from rural to urban life. Although not a mass membership organization like the NAACP and other civil rights
groups, the League's concern for the urban Negro has played
an important part in the latter's orientation and adjustment to
city life. Led by Whitney Young, Jr., the League's Executive
Director, important programs in social welfare, on-the-job
training, housing and education have been carried out quietly
and effectively. There is an Urban League office in almost
every city with a large Negro population.

The year 1942 saw the founding, in Chicago, of the Con-

These three Civil Rights workers were murdered in Mississippi in June of 1964. Left to right: Andrew Goodman, James Chaney, and Michael Schwerner. *(CORE)*

gress of Racial Equality, but it was not until the 1950's that this group began to reach national proportions. Its first leader and founder was James Farmer under whose militant leadership CORE moved into the forefront of the civil rights struggle. In 1961, CORE initiated a new technique. It sent hundreds of volunteers into the South to test segregation laws in interstate transportation and terminal facilities. These protesters became known as "Freedom Riders." Led by Farmer himself, the Freedom Riders numbered, at times, more than one thousand Negroes and whites. The final result was the desegregation of interstate transportation and the rise of a new force of militant, non-violent protesters. In February 1966 Farmer left his post of leadership to take a leading position in the newly founded National Center for Community Action and Education, Inc.

By 1960 there was a stirring among many young people throughout the nation. The call went out for a new and dynamic militancy which would not be satisfied with words and promises. Their call was "Freedom Now" and not tomorrow. For this group, even the more radical civil rights movements like CORE were not enough and thus, in 1960, various student protest groups founded SNCC (popularly called "SNICK"), the Student Non-Violent Coordinating Committee. The original meeting was called by Dr. King, but the students felt his proposals were too moderate. The new student movement directed its action to the heart of the nation's problem. Its members moved in to live and work with the people who were (and are) being denied their freedom. Most of their limited money and personnel has been directed toward the South where the problems are most pressing, but their militancy has spread to all parts of the country. They bring with them a dedication and energy which is aimed at awakening the poor and oppressed. They have shown, and continue to show themselves willing to accept the same hardships and suffering of the people they try to help. They have faced violence, jail, and even death to bring freedom to the Negro. They have been a moving force behind the drive for equal rights in public accommodations, making wide use of the now famous "sit-in" technique. More recently, they have fought, along with other civil rights workers, for voting rights and for economic and social, non-violent revolution among the Negroes and whites of this country.

Another View of Race Relations: The Black Muslims

The Black Muslims have been, for the last ten years, one of the most controversial black nationalist groups in America. The center of the movement is Chicago, where its present leader, Elijah Muhammad, "Spiritual Head of the Muslims in the West," lives and directs "the faithful." There are temples in almost every major city in America. They have had, until recently, particularly strong support in New York City, Philadelphia, Los Angeles, and Chicago.

The movement had its beginnings in 1930. A Muslim known as W. D. Fard, whose origins are unknown, appeared in Detroit and began teaching his own brand of Islamism. The major tenets of his teaching were that the white man and the white man's religion—Christianity—are evil; and that the black man, by following Fard's interpretation of the religion of Islam, is destined to destroy the "white devils," at some future Battle of Armageddon. The movement grew slowly, at first gaining some support among Negroes in the Northern "Black Ghettoes."

Providence Baptist Church, one of two destroyed by fire in the early morning of August 3, 1965, near Slidell, Louisiana. (CORE)

Three years after Fard founded the movement, he vanished. There is as little information about his disappearance as there is about his appearance in Detroit three years earlier. He was succeeded by one of his closest assistants, Elijah Muhammad, born Elijah Poole. Muhammad still directs the movement from his headquarters in Chicago, although his public appearances are less frequent than formerly. Under his leadership the movement grew from two to seventy or eighty mosques. Following a strict policy of isolation from the white man's world, the Black Muslims have established their own temples and schools, apartment houses and stores, restaurants and farms. Closely connected with this system of isolation is the conviction that they are more than the equals of the white man. They are "Black men" with a manifest destiny under the leadership of a black god.

Although the Black Muslims officially maintain that they avoid bloodshed, they have periodically been involved in outbreaks of violence. They are strict believers in the doctrine of an "eye for an eye," and each Muslim vows to avenge himself for any overt aggression against himself or any of his "brothers."

Since 1964, however, the Black Muslims have been losing ground and schisms have developed within the movement. Much of their appeal to the traditional Negro hatred of white society has been lessened as the non-violent civil rights groups have helped to bring about improved conditions and relations with the white community. As the leaders of Federal, state, and local governments have given way to the spirit of change, many Negroes have begun to hope that there are better answers to their problems than a chauvinistic separatism.

Malcolm X

Perhaps the most striking and interesting figure to emerge from the Black Muslim movement was Malcolm X. In his short career he became the most articulate spokesman for the Black Muslims and for the many smaller black nationalist organizations.

Malcolm X was born Malcolm Little, one of eleven children, in Omaha, Nebraska, about 1925. Later, the family moved to Lansing, Michigan, where his father, a Baptist minister, soon incurred the hostility of his white neighbors because he was so outspoken on racial issues. Malcolm was only six when the family home was burned by the Ku Klux Klan and his father doggedly rebuilt it in the same neighborhood. In what appeared to be an accident, Mr. Little was killed. Malcolm, however, always believed he was murdered by his white enemies. The bitterness of these early years remained with Malcolm until the last years before his murder.

Malcolm X's life was an interesting one. From Lansing he went to Harlem where he learned the ins and outs of the dope racket, the numbers game, bootlegging whiskey, and diverse forms of hustling. He was finally arrested and jailed in the maximum security prison at Concord, Massachusetts. In 1947, while in prison, Malcolm was converted by one of his brothers who had become a member of Muhammad's Detroit Temple. From then, until his split with the movement and Elijah Muhammad in 1964, Malcolm gave all his time and energies to the Black Muslims. When he left the Black Muslims, he tried to build a new movement based on his unique and still-developing philosophy of race relations, human rights, and revolution. In his view, the white man and the white power structure were still the enemy. But he now felt it was possible to work with civil rights groups to solve some of the most pressing problems facing the Negro. And, he conceded, it was also possible for whites to join with him if they could completely accept the necessity for eventual revolution and overthrow of the white power structure. If, that is, they could give up the psychological fact of their whiteness.

Malcolm X is a symbol of the two alternatives Americans face today: a peaceful solution to the racial problem, with Negroes and whites working earnestly together; or hatred, violence, and open warfare.

In 1963, as the civil rights movement gained momentum, a vast new wave of militancy swept across the United States. A Department of Justice study indicates that in one twelve-week period, 1,412 separate civil rights demonstrations took place. Birmingham, Alabama, was one of the main targets of protest, and Dr. King led demonstrations against what he called "the most thoroughly segregated city in the United States." The Birmingham protest became violent when more than 2,000 Negroes marched on the downtown section of the city and Public Safety Commissioner "Bull" Connor ordered high-powered fire hoses and snarling police dogs used against the demonstrators.

The atrocities spread. William Moore, a postal employee, was shot to death on an Alabama highway as he staged a one-man "Freedom Walk." In Mississippi, NAACP Field Secretary Medgar Evers was assassinated as he entered his home.

And in Birmingham, Alabama, four Negro girls were blown to pieces when their Sunday School was bombed; later the same day, two other youngsters were shot to death.

The increased demonstrations and the accompanying violence of 1963 reached such intensity that President Kennedy decided new laws were needed to provide Negroes with a remedy other than street demonstrations. The President called the situation a "moral crisis" for America, and asked Congress to enact a sweeping omnibus Civil Rights Act aimed at lifting the Negro from legalized second-class citizenship.

The 1963 civil rights struggle reached its high point on August 28th when nearly a quarter of a million whites and Negroes participated in a March on Washington. Gathering at the Lincoln Memorial, the throng heard Roy Wilkins, Whitney Young, labor leader A. Phillip Randolph, CORE's James Farmer, and others articulate the hopes and dreams of most Americans. But it was Dr. King who provided what was generally acclaimed the most moving statement of the Negro's hopes and aspirations:

> I have a dream that one day, on the red hills of Georgia, sons of former slaves and the sons of former slaveowners will be able to sit down together at the table of brotherhood.
> I have a dream that one day even the state of Mississippi, a state sweltering with the heat of injustice, sweltering with the heat of oppression, will be transformed into an oasis of freedom and justice.
> I have a dream that my little children will one day live in a nation where they will not be judged by the color of their skin but by the content of their character. . . .

On Friday, November 22, 1963, an assassin killed John F. Kennedy, the 35th President of the United States. The murder occurred in Dallas, Texas, but its impact was felt throughout the world. For leaders of the civil rights movement, it loomed as an especially tragic loss. But what President Kennedy had sought to accomplish during his too-brief term in the White House was taken up by President Johnson. Although Southern Senators, many of whom had served with Johnson in the Senate, tried to kill the pending Civil Rights Act by a traditional filibuster, more responsible Senators prevailed. On July 2, 1964, President Johnson signed the bill into operative law.

The 1964 Civil Rights Act deals with a variety of public and private matters affecting Negro and white citizens. The law forbids racial discrimination in publicly-owned-and-operated facilities, and in most privately-owned places of public accommodation, such as motels, restaurants, cinemas. The law gives the Attorney General of the United States authority to *begin* civil suits in behalf of victims of discrimination. The act forbids voting registrars from discriminating against qualified Negroes seeking to register and vote. In addition, the law created a Commission to investigate alleged racial discrimination by employers and labor unions.

But while the time-consuming procedures of Congress were producing this major civil rights legislation, contrary forces were not idle. From July to September 1964, a series of apparently spontaneous but massive riots occurred in major cities in the North. The fatal shooting of a fifteen-year-old Negro schoolboy, James Powell, by a New York City police lieutenant set off riots in Harlem and Brooklyn. Rochester, New York; Jersey City, New Jersey; Dixmoor, Illinois (just outside Chicago); and Philadelphia, Pennsylvania, were all subjected to days and nights of attempted mob rule. Investigations that followed the riots indicated clearly that the rioters and looters included many youngsters who were out of work and caught up in the hot and desperate hopelessness that is symptomatic of the Black Ghetto. New York City's then Mayor Robert F. Wagner described them as having no roots in the past and no hopes for the future. For all its truth, this was a very sad commentary for the mayor of our largest city to have to make.

There was one particularly brutal chapter in the 1964 civil rights year. Three young civil rights workers, two whites and a Negro, were part of a Council of Federated Organizations (COFO) summer project working in Mississippi. Andrew Goodman and Michael Schwerner of New York (both white), and James Chaney, a Negro from Meridian, Mississippi, disappeared in mid-June. FBI agents discovered their burned and abandoned station wagon a few days later. But it was not until August that the FBI found the trio's decomposed bodies buried under an earthen dam on a remote farm. All three had been shot, and one physician who examined the bodies reported that Chaney had been mutilated. Approximately twenty-two white men were charged with taking part in the murders, but the charges brought by the Federal government were restricted to civil rights violations because murder is not a Federal offense unless committed on Federal property. Most of the twenty-two men charged escaped any court action and the case went down in history as another tragic event on the road to freedom.

With the 1964 Civil Rights Act on the statute books, 1965 became a year of tactical change in the civil rights movement. Emphasis shifted from desegregating public facilities to political action, especially in the South. Dr. King selected Selma, Alabama, as a prime target because the city provided a classic example of a potential majority of eligible Negro voters who were prevented from voting by a white minority. Repeated attempts to get Negroes registered in Selma met with persistent frustration at the hands of local officials. Demonstrations availed nothing as the local sheriff, James Clark, made it plain that he intended to fill the city's jails with Negro demonstrators as fast as he could lay hands on them. Selma Public Safety Director, Wilson Baker, took a more moderate stand, but Clark had the open support of Alabama's segregationist governor, George Wallace.

On Sunday, March 7, several hundred Negroes tried to begin a protest march from Selma to the state capital of Montgomery, about fifty miles away. Mounted State Police and Sheriff Clark's deputies unleased a brutal attack on the Negroes; tear gas, bull whips, cattle prods, and clubs were used against men, women, and children. The Negroes were beaten back, fresh evidence of Alabama's interpretation of "the Southern way of life." The Department of Justice entered the case and, with civil rights leaders, petitioned for an injunction against Alabama officials who had tried to prevent the march.

Shortly before a Federal judge ruled on the petitions, thousands of Negroes and whites began converging on Selma from every section of the country. Many of those who came to participate in the historic march were religious leaders, clergymen, and nuns. One of them, the Rev. James Reeb, a Unitarian minister from Boston, Massachusetts, was attacked and beaten by four white men; he died a few days later.

> I speak tonight for the dignity of man and the destiny of democracy. I urge every member of both parties, Americans of all religions and of all colors, from every section of this country, to join me in that cause. At times, history and fate meet in a single time in a single place to shape a turning point in man's unending search for freedom. So it was at Lexington and Concord. So it was a century ago at Appomattox. So it was last week in Selma, Alabama.

With those words, President Johnson began an address to Congress and the American people on March 15, 1965. The events in Selma had gouged deep and searing scars in both the American conscience and the American image throughout the world. It was clearly a moment in history when courage and leadership of the highest order were required. Lyndon Baines Johnson, newly elected to a four-year term, and with landslide mandate to boot, stood ready to exhibit courage and exercise moral leadership. After announcing that he would submit a voting rights bill to the Congress, the President added that the new law "will provide for citizens to be registered by officials of the United States Government, if the state officials refuse to register them."

For the next few days, the Selma-to-Montgomery Freedom March occupied the world's attention. Whites and Negroes walked and sang their way along Highway 82 while Federal troops and Alabama National Guardsmen kept watch. Journalists covering the event reported that the people who marched were firm in their hopes that what they were doing would somehow help to make a better America.

But the Selma-to-Montgomery march was to have a tragic postscript. Just a few hours after the march ended, Mrs. Viola Liuzzo, a white Detroit housewife and mother, was shuttling some of the marchers back to Selma in her automobile. Suddenly, and without warning, a car loaded with white men approached and gunshots rang out. Several slugs penetrated the woman's body and killed her. The four killers were members of the Ku Klux Klan. An all-white jury found them not guilty.

Long Hot Summer: 1965

In "the long hot summer" of 1965, when riots were sweeping many cities throughout the nation, it was hard to predict where the next outburst would come. Negroes living in Los Angeles had for years been almost unanimous in their denunciations of racial policies there. It was not, then, a great surprise when the most widespread and violent riot in the history of the United States wracked that city for several days in the summer of 1965. It began in the Negro ghetto of Los Angeles known as Watts. Watts is a 72-square-mile area that houses ninety per cent of Los Angeles County's 600,000 Negroes. It is a ghetto that has grown steadily with the migration of Negroes into Los Angeles from the South. In Watts, the streets are tree-lined and the houses are primarily one- or two-family houses. Behind this facade, however, is the same poverty, discontent, and desperate hopelessness that is common to the slum ghettos of New York, Chicago, Philadephia, and other major urban communities; the same growing bitterness over the treatment of Negroes at the hands of politicians, educators, and police; the same feeling of being shut out from jobs and education; the same feeling of being forever pushed to the bottom of the heap.

On Wednesday, August 11, 1965, at 7:45 p.m., the spark was ignited. Two highway patrol officers stopped a car and arrested its twenty-one-year-old Negro driver, Marquette Frye, and his brother. The young Negroes' mother soon arrived on the scene from their nearby home, and an argument developed between the Fryes and the white police officers. Crowds grew around the scene and the police failed to disperse them or to resolve quickly enough what had begun as a routine arrest for "drunken driving." The crowd accused the police of using unnecessary force. As words were exchanged and the crowd continued to grow, tempers boiled over, rocks were thrown, and some youths became more violent. When the police failed in their attempts to break up the crowd, it began moving sullenly through the streets. Soon it was clear that a full-scale riot was on.

The riot lasted six days, August 11-16. Entire blocks were burned and hundreds of stores were looted. Gun shops and pawnshops were raided for arms and ammunition. Anything that moved became a target—even airplanes. When the rioting was over, thirty-five people had been killed and hundreds had been injured. Twenty-eight of the dead were Negroes. Property damage in the hundred and fifty-block area exceeded 200,000,000 dollars.

On March 14, 1966, there was new violence in Watts. As the McCone Commission appointed by the governor to investigate the August riots had warned, they would be a mere "curtain raiser" for future violence unless a "revolutionary attitude" was adopted toward racial problems.

The problems in Watts are by no means solved, nor are the problems in other communities throughout the country. It is clear that continually temporizing our racial problems is an invitation to disaster.

It is hard to say just when the "Negro pilgrimage" came to an end. Nobody can set the exact date or the hour, but when the hope and the expectation for the peaceful pursuit of the blessings of liberty began to fade into uncertainty, something beautiful and something vital died in America. That hope began to dim when the Eighty-Ninth Congress closed the books without any new civil rights legislation in 1965. In a sense, no new legislation was needed, for in theory the laws we have are adequate to protect the rights of all American citizens. In practice, the laws discriminate—or they permit discrimination. A black American may not always enjoy the privileges of an American who is white:

> Blacks and whites together
> Separate in stormy weather.

The Negro pilgrimage was a journey of faith—faith in God, faith in the democratic process and faith in the essential good-

Dr. Martin Luther King, Jr., in Memphis, Tennessee on April 4, 1968, the day before he was assassinated. (*World Wide Photos*)

ness, the social morality of the American people. The steady, peaceful pursuit of the enjoyment of rights already implicit in their citizenship and in our basic Constitution, symbolized the courageousness of American blacks, no less than their patience and their commitment to peaceful social change. Their pilgrimage always welcomed the encouragement and participation of the white brother who placed his own life and fortune on the line for the black man's cause, and for the larger cause of justice in a democratic society. The Negro pilgrimage was a painful odyssey, and its accomplishments were notable. It is a reflection upon how tenuously we hold our commitments to the principles of democracy that the gains that were made always needed to be reconfirmed in law—statute law. For most Americans, their "constitutional rights" (and the constitutional rights of others) are rather nebulous abstractions. New laws on the books, if they do no more than restate what is clearly stated in the Constitution, provide a "present" relevance for those who have forgotten what the law was, and for those who need to have the law recognized and honored in the breach. That is why the failure of Congress to support with legislation the valiant struggles of American citizens for freedom in free America was a bitter and disillusioning experience. And that is why the freedom of all Americans is always in potential danger. We do not know the strengths, nor do we know the limitations, of democracy because we have practiced it so seldom.

In 1965 and 1966 the arena of civil rights protest shifted from the South to the great cities and the pleasant suburbs of the North. When this happened, there was a noticeable falling away of support from whites who had been sympathetic to the movement. Money to mount the demonstrations and protests was increasingly difficult to come by. In Chicago and Milwaukee and Cleveland and Rochester—all over the North—white hostility to the black search for reasonable participation in the good life in America was quite as pronounced as in the South. White Americans in the North wanted "their" *public* schools kept "white"—just as they did in the South. They wanted black people barred from buying houses in "their" neighborhood. The lily white craft unions in New York and Philadelphia remained closed to Negro applicants just as they were in Birmingham and Jackson, Mississippi. The best paying jobs in the corporations, the banks, the airlines and the communications media in the North had "white" specifications, however subliminal, just as they did in

People among the charred ruins of their home in Detroit after the 1967 riots. (*World Wide Photos*)

Members of the Black Panthers outside the Alameda County Court House, Oakland, in August, 1968, during the Huey Newton trial. (*World Wide Photos*)

the South. The Yankee indignation at the unbridled savagery with which the South had met the peaceful protests of Martin Luther King, James Farmer and their followers, turned to petulance when black protest came to Boston; and mayhem when they tried to take freedom to Cicero. The Negro pilgrimage had gone too far. The civil rights movement ground to a halt. The Poor People's March on Washington would be the final effort to recapture the romance of "black and white together" in search of the American Dream for everybody. The "Poor People" (blacks and whites and a few Indians for good measure) could not bring it off. Suddenly, the war in Vietnam claimed everybody's attention and everyone's energy. The cause of freedom at home would have to wait. Again. At that point something died in America. Something great. Something vital.

Frustration laid hold on black America and her convulsions shook the country. There was a progressive shift from a non-violent, Christian-oriented ideology to a new more pragmatic perspective—"freedom now—*by any means necessary!*" Not all Negroes were willing to abandon faith in non-violence. Many did. The "long, hot summer" became a euphemism for riot. The black ghettoes of the Northern cities were put to the torch: Newark, Detroit, New York, Washington and scores of others. White merchants lost their goods; black residents were burned out. People were killed; almost all of them were black. Thousands were jailed; hundreds were injured. The police, the National Guard and the Army occupied the black ghettoes and patrolled the streets. Suddenly there was hatred. There had always been fear.

Black leadership was divided. Some leaders like Roy Wilkins of the NAACP called for "sanity"—the recognition that the black minority needed the white majority to win its freedom, and that freedom could not be won by violence in the streets. Others, like Stokely Carmichael, urged a total commitment to "black power," a term which was given a free and convenient interpretation by a wide spectrum of its devotees. Martin Luther King, whose commitment to love as an instrument of social change had won the world's acclaim, refused under the most extraordinary provocation to consider violence as an acceptable response to the violence of others, or as an expedient to move society toward the recognition of basic human rights for Blackamericans.

On April 4, 1968, Martin Luther King was murdered in Memphis, Tennessee. Martin Luther King was a dreamer, and

Julian Bond, leader of the insurgent Georgia delegation to the 1968 Democratic National Convention in Chicago. (*World Wide Photos*)

his dream was that the America he loved so much would some day be able to accept the people he loved so much; and that Americans would be one people. One *great* people. Martin Luther King's dream was that love would be the efficient cause, the instrument for bringing the true community into being—in America. They killed Doctor King—society has always killed its dreamers. But did they kill the dream? It is the same dream that held the Negro pilgrimage together, that sustained the Negro pilgrims against impossible odds on a hundred year search for freedom. Why did the dream have to die?

American Negroes have often been criticized for not being like "the Jews," or "the Irish," or "the Italians." They have been told to "stay with your own kind," and "pull yourselves up by your own bootstraps." Sometimes Negroes trying to escape the ghetto have been asked, "If *you* don't want to be with Negroes, why should we want to be with *you*?" Even Booker T. Washington advised his followers: "Let down your buckets where you are." Implicit in all these arguments is the suspicion that black people secretly hate themselves, and that they want to escape into the "white" world. It is probable that most black people have known self-hatred at one time or another. In a society which extols all that is associated with white people and ridicules whatever is associated with black people, it is difficult to imagine that self-hatred could be avoided completely. That is the tragedy confronting all black children: the lack of acceptable positive values with which to

Representative Shirley Chisholm, the first black woman elected to Congress. (*World Wide Photos*)

identify. Whatever is available to them is negated by the over-culture and regarded as improper, immoral, ugly or of no account.

Nevertheless, the desire to "escape" into the white world is not necessarily an attempt to escape from one's friends and associates or from one's own subculture. It is fundamentally an attempt to escape *to* opportunity and *from* oppression. The suggestion that the fortunes of the Afro-Americans could be substantially improved by "being like" the Euro-Americans ignores a very crucial factor that is not ignored at any other time—namely: the Afro-Americans are black; the Euro-Americans are white; and in America, color makes a critical difference. The life chances of the typical black American are structured by the color of his skin, and no amount of "boot-strapping" or "being like" the Irish or the Jews or the Italians is going to significantly affect the consequences of that fact.

In 1968 the National Advisory Commission on Civil Disorders, after an exhaustive study, reported to President Johnson that America "is a racist society." If that is true, the answers to our racial dilemma would seem to lie in changing behaviors and attitudes somewhere else other than in the black community. Perhaps we should *all* be like the Jews, the Irish and the Italians! It is undemocratic, of course, to require any ethnic group to be like anybody other than themselves. It is unrealistic to expect that they will—or can—or want to. The potential greatness of America is her potential for tolerating and encouraging healthy subcultures while building a national culture to which every ethnic group contributes, and which represents the cultural common denominator in which every American participates and finds his national identity.

The Negro pilgrimage saw, with Martin Luther King, "the mountaintop" from a distance. It had run its logical course, and with the old tools and strategies, could go no further. The last mile between slavery and freedom is a mile the man who would be truly free has to walk alone with himself. Others may help break the chains. A man has to free himself. Freedom moves from the inside out; not from the outside in.

One of the odd features about the black experience in America has been the fact the Negroes have never been a true ethnic group. They wanted to move from slavery to freedom, from Africans to Americans without even being *Afro-Americans*! If the challenge to "be like the Jews," etc., is America's way of recommending the ethnic experience as a kind of cultural seasoning rather than an implied denigration of the

Tommie Smith, center, and John Carlos in racial protest during playing of "The Star Spangled Banner," after receiving their gold and bronze medals at the 1968 Olympic Games. (*World Wide Photos*)

Stokely Carmichael speaking at
the University of Texas in April,
1969. (*World Wide Photos*)

black experience itself, then America, (since it is a veritable nation of ethnic groups), ought to be heard. There is very good evidence that the ethnic process is the institutionalized formula for transition in ·America. It has a conditioning effect upon the ethnic group and upon the over-culture, preparing them, as it were, for each other.

The contemporary "black revolution" is the overt expression of the black man's discovery of himself and his ethnic group. He is not a "Negro" anymore; he is an Afro-American or a Blackamerican. In the rejection of the appellation "Negro" he is trying desperately to communicate something more than a projection of his own self-image. He wants to signify his newly discovered ethnic spirit. He is a *black* man—not necessarily in color, but in affiliation. He belongs to a community of black men—a black sub-culture. Yet he is American, because despite the discrimination which limits his participation in the social process, he logically and properly belongs to (and has made important contributions to), the national culture. His sub-culture is "Blackamerican." His national culture, like his national political status, is "American."

Learning ethnicity is a new experience for the Blackamerican. It means a reassessment of cultural priorities. It is not easy for Negro leaders and others who have spent a lifetime struggling to be "accepted" by white people and the white power structure to now be willing to defer acceptance while they learn how to be "black." Some Negroes will never learn to be black, nor is it reasonable to expect them to. But the options are not reduced to learning ethnicity *or* being "accepted." The pertinent genius of an ethnic group is that it has built-in structures which provide for the psychological (if not the economic) security of its members who do not find full acceptance in the over-culture. An ethnic group is literally a big family. It nurtures its own and provides appreciation and understanding until transition is accomplished. In the language of the black revolution, the ethnic spirit is expressed in "soul," a conscious affinity for the black experience, and an appreciation of its unique traditions—its travail and its accomplishments.

The New Blacks—the black youth of the contemporary generation—have soul. They are proud to be black; proud to be a part of the black experience. They have discovered that *black is beautiful*, and they want other Americans to have an appreciation of that fact. The New Blacks have demanded that the history, the art and the literature of Blackamericans be taught in the schools and colleges. This is a reasonable expectation. Blackamericans helped this country to be what it is. Its history is in part their history. Their history, their art, their literature are a vital part of American culture. The academic curricula should reflect this fact with becoming integrity. Americans, black and white, need broader, more realistic perspectives on the development of the country they share, and must continue to share as one nation. Indivisible.

Supreme Court Justice Thurgood Marshall. (*World Wide Photos*)

Chronology

1492

Pedro Alonzo Niño, Negro navigator of the Niña, reaches New World with Columbus. Negro explorers also figured prominently in the expeditions led by Balboa, Cortez, Navarez, and the Jesuit-led French parties that explored Canada and the upper portions of the Mississippi River.

1619

Twenty Negroes purchased by the English colonists of Jamestown, Virginia, to serve as bondsmen.

1662

Virginia legislature enacts law declaring all children of mixed unions to be slave or free according to the status of the mother only.

1663-1864

At least 109 slave revolts occur on land, with 55 taking place on slave ships at sea between 1699 and 1845.

1664

Maryland enacts law enslaving freeborn white women married to Negro slaves, and the children of such marriages. Later repealed to prevent forced marriages of white servants to slaves.

1667

Virginia repeals her earlier statute enfranchising Negroes who converted to Christianity.

1682

Virginia law reduces all non-Christian bondsmen to permanent slave status regardless of any later religious conversion.

1712

Massive slave uprisings in New York City.

1715-1750

Slave importations for all the colonies jump from 2,500 to 7,500 per year.

1731

Birth of Benjamin Banneker, Negro scientist and mathematician, appointed by George Washington to help survey and lay out the District of Columbia.

1739

Three massive slave revolts take place in South Carolina.

1752

First manumission statute enacted by Maryland.

1753

Birth, in Africa, of Phillis Wheatley, famous Negro poetess of New England.

1770

Death of Negro sailor, Crispus Attucks, in Boston Massacre, March 5. Considered to be first martyr of American Revolution.

1773

Publication of Phillis Wheatley's *Poems on Various Subjects, Religious and Moral,* shortly after her manumission.

1774

Thomas Jefferson and Benjamin Franklin help convince Continental Congress to bar the importation of slaves after December 1, 1775.

1775

As commander of the Continental Army, George Washington orders all Negroes excluded from service in war. Later forced to modify his position, Washington accepts free Negroes but persists in barring slaves.

Two Negroes, Peter Salem and Salem Poor, emerge as heroes from Battle of Bunker Hill. They were among 5,000 Negro soldiers to serve in Continental Army.

1776

Despite Thomas Jefferson's plea, Continental Congress refuses to make abolition a part of the Declaration of Independence, thus denying the Negro a stake in the ideals outlined in that document.

1782

Negro slave population of Virginia reaches 260,000.

1787

Founding Fathers provide for a twenty-year extension of the slave trade in drafting Constitution.

1792

Eli Whitney invents cotton gin. This is followed by a great rise in demand for slave labor to meet the needs of the expanding cotton industry.

1793

First of two Federal fugitive slave laws enacted.

1800

Gabriel Prosser and Jack Bowler lead eleven hundred fellow slaves to attack Richmond, Virginia. Prosser, Bowler, and others executed after betrayal of plot.

Denmark Vesey, a freed Negro, organizes plot to seize Charleston. Plan fails because of betrayal, 139 Negroes are arrested. Vesey and 47 others are executed.

1803

Louisiana Purchase opens new areas for cultivation and provides foundation for doctrine of "Manifest Destiny."

1807-1838

New York, Pennsylvania, New Jersey, and Connecticut enact laws disenfranchising Negroes or abridging their voting rights as a response to the Northern migration following enactment of Southern manumission laws.

1808

Slave trade *officially* outlawed in America, relegating the still-active industry to unofficial status.

1815

Return of veterans from War of 1812 bringing news of freedom to be found in Canada marks the beginning of the Underground Railroad.

1817

American Colonization Society forms, to settle freed Negroes in what is now Liberia.

1820

Missouri Compromise prohibits slavery north of the southern boundary of Missouri.

First ship carrying Negroes from America to Liberia leaves America, February 6. Arrives in Sierra Leone, March 9.

1827

First Negro newspaper, *Freedom's Journal,* founded in New York City by John B. Russwurm.

1830

Federal census reports 3,777 Negro family heads as slaveholders.

1830-1860

By popular estimate, two thousand Negroes per year travel the Underground Railroad to freedom.

1831

Nat Turner leads fellow slaves in Southampton County [Virginia] Insurrection. Fifty-nine white men, women, and children are murdered. Turner captured and executed.

1835

William Lloyd Garrison, abolitionist editor of *The Liberator,* attacked and beaten by white Bostonians.

1844

Baptists divide over sending slaveholding missionaries into the expanding Southwest.

1847

Taxable income of free Negroes in Philadelphia estimated at $400,000.

1849

Charles Sumner pioneers by introducing the concept of equal protection under law into a racial controversy in *Roberts v. City of Boston.*

1850

Compromise of 1850 sets up balanced set of conditions for the future admission of new states.

Thirty-seven per cent of free Negro population classified as mulattoes.

1852

Publication of Harriet Beecher Stowe's *Uncle Tom's Cabin,* March 20, 1852. This work had a major influence on the attitudes of Americans toward the problem of slavery and became a classic in its own time. The book gives a moving account of the evils and brutality of slavery.

1856

Pro-slavery forces raid and sack Lawrence, Kansas, May 21, thus beginning two years of violence in Kansas that cost more than 200 lives.

1857

In *Scott v. Sanford* (Dred Scott Decision), U.S. Supreme Court proclaims slavery a national concept and states that Negroes have "no rights a white man need respect."

1859

John Brown attacks U.S. arsenal at Harper's Ferry, Virginia, October 16. Counterattack, led by Col. Robert E. Lee, results in Brown's capture and his execution on December 2.

1860

Abraham Lincoln elected President of the United States.

South Carolina secedes from the Union, December 18, followed by Florida, Alabama, Mississippi, Louisiana, Texas.

1861

Confederate forces fire on Fort Sumter in Charleston Harbor, April 11.

Congress passes Confiscation Act freeing slaves under Union Army control who had previously been used to aid the Confederacy.

1862

Without official authorization, Union General David Hunter organizes first all-Negro regiment, the First South Carolina Volunteers.

Congress passes second Confiscation Act granting freedom to all slaves of masters supporting the Confederacy, July 17.

President Lincoln issues preliminary Emancipation Proclamation, September 22.

First authorized Negro combat units, the First Regiment Louisiana Heavy Artillery and the Massachusetts Fifty-fourth and Fifty-fifth Infantry Regiments, are organized.

1862-1865

Two hundred thousand Negroes serve in the Union Army, of whom 38,000 give their lives. Twenty-two Negroes are awarded Congressional Medals of Honor.

1863

President Lincoln issues Emancipation Proclamation freeing slaves in rebel states, January 1.

Active recruitment of Negro soldiers for the Union Army begins under designation *United States Colored Troops* or USCT.

1864

Congress passes bill granting Negro soldiers the same pay as white troops.

On April 12, Confederate General Nathan Forrest and his troops capture the Union stronghold at Fort Pillow, near Memphis, Tennessee, and murder every Negro they find— half the garrison.

1865

Congress passes the Thirteenth Amendment to the Constitution, abolishing slavery in America, January 31; ratified December 18.

General Lee surrenders at Appomattox Courthouse, ending the Civil War, April 9.

Abraham Lincoln assassinated, in Washington, D. C., April 15.

White legislatures in former rebel states issue "Black Codes" restricting the rights and freedom of movement of freedmen.

Confederate General Nathan B. Forrest organizes the Ku Klux Klan.

1866

Civil Rights Act, granting Negroes Federal protection in certain social situations and against physical violence, passed by Congress over President Andrew Johnson's veto.

1867

Congress passes First Reconstruction Act in March, dividing the former Confederacy into five districts under military rule. Also required that the states ratify the "Civil War Amendments," give Negroes the vote, and hold new elections for state offices.

1868

Fourteenth Amendment to the Constitution, granting Negroes full citizenship, ratified July 28.

1869-1880

Twenty-two Negroes serve in U.S. House of Representatives.

1870

The Fifteenth Amendment, granting Negroes the right to vote, becomes part of the Constitution, March 30.

Hiram R. Revels of Mississippi becomes first Negro U.S. senator, February 25. Negro senator, Blanche K. Bruce, also of Mississippi, elected, March 5, 1875.

1873

In *Slaughterhouse Cases,* U.S. Supreme Court rules that "due process" clause of the Fourteenth Amendment only grants protection of *national,* not of state, citizenship rights.

1875

Congress enacts Civil Rights Bill giving Negroes right to equal treatment in inns, public conveyances, and places of public amusement, March 1.

1876

Reconstruction ends with the election of Rutherford B. Hayes to the Presidency. Hayes withdraws all remaining Northern troops from the South.

In *United States v. Cruikshank,* U.S. Supreme Court rules against punishing persons who broke up a Negro political meeting on the grounds that the meeting did not concern a National Election.

1883

In the *Civil Rights Cases,* U.S. Supreme Court strikes down sections of the 1875 Civil Rights Act that prohibit discrimination in places of public accommodation.

1888

First Negro bank, the Savings Bank of the Grand Fountain Order of True Reformers, founded in Richmond, Virginia.

1888-1934

One hundred and thirty-four Negro-controlled banks organized.

1895

Booker T. Washington sets forth the "separate fingers doctrine," calling upon Negroes to gain advantages through work, not by militating for social equality.

1896

In *Plessy v. Ferguson,* U.S. Supreme Court establishes the "separate but equal" doctrine, May 18.

1898

Widespread outbreaks of racial violence erupt, punctuated by riots, lynchings, and the progressive disenfranchisement of Negroes.

1903

Publication of Dr. W. E. B. DuBois' *The Souls of Black Folks.*

1905

Thirty prominent Negroes, led by Dr. W. E. B. DuBois, meet at Fort Erie, Canada, July 29, and found the "Niagara Movement," dedicated to "aggressive action" on behalf of Negro freedom and growth. (Movement evolved into NAACP.)

Robert S. Abbott publishes first issue of *The Defender.*

1909

National Association for the Advancement of Colored People [NAACP] founded, February 12.

Dr. William A. Attaway organizes first Negro legal reserve life insurance company, the Mississippi Life Insurance Company.

1910

National Urban League organized in New York.

1914

Lynchings and floggings of Negroes number 1,100, most of which take place in the North.

1915

Great Migration begins as a result of Southern crop failures and World War I manpower drainage.

Death of Booker T. Washington.

1917

America enters World War I, April 6, and stops accepting Negro volunteers. Navy begins a quarter century policy of discrimination against Negro servicemen.

Selected Service Act reopens Negro Army inductions as enlisted men.

Six hundred and thirty-nine Negroes graduate first all-Negro officer training school, October 15.

Publication of James Weldon Johnson's *Fifty Years and Other Poems*.

1918

World War I armistice signed. Over 371,000 Negroes served in War, of whom more than half served in France. The all-Negro 369th Infantry Regiment, or "Hell Fighters," was awarded the *Croix de Guerre*, and Private Henry Johnson of that regiment was the first American decorated by the French with the *Croix de Guerre*.

1919

More than twenty race riots rock the United States in a six-month period, the worst of which take place in Washington, D. C., July 19, and Chicago, July 27. Period becomes known as "the Red Summer."

1923

Membership in Marcus Garvey's black nationalist Universal Negro Improvement Association reaches over half a million.

1925

A. Phillip Randolph organizes Brotherhood of Sleeping Car Porters and Maids.

1927

Marcus Garvey deported as undesirable alien.

1929

Stock market collapse, October 29, adversely affecting a vast number of already poverty-stricken Negroes.

1930

Black Muslim movement founded by W. D. Fard, in Detroit.

1934

Elijah Muhammad takes over leadership of the Black Muslim movement and consolidates his power from his new headquarters in Chicago.

1935

Willard Townsend begins to organize United Transport Service Employees.

Maryland Court of Appeals orders University of Maryland to admit Negro law student Donald Murray.

1935-1945

Negro union membership jumps from 180,000 to 1,250,-
000.

1937

William H. Hastic becomes Judge of Federal District
Court in Virgin Islands, first Negro Federal Judge, March
26.

1938

Supreme Court orders the admission of Lloyd Gaines, a
Negro, to University of Missouri Law School.

1939

Hattie McDaniel wins "Oscar" for her portrayal of a
Negro slave in *Gone With the Wind*.

1941

First class of Negro pilots graduated from segregated
aviation school at Tuskegee Army Air Field, March 7.

Robert C. Weaver becomes director of a section in the
Office of Production Management devoted to integrating
Negroes into national defense program, April 18.

Negro seaman Dorie Miller shoots down six of the Japanese bombers attacking Pearl Harbor, December 7. Receives Navy Cross, May 27, 1942.

President Franklin D. Roosevelt issues Executive Order
8802, providing for anti-discrimination clauses in all defense contracts and establishing a Fair Employment
Practices Commission in the Office of Production Management, June 25.

1942

All-Negro 332nd Fighter Group activated under the command of Negro Colonel Benjamin O. Davis, Jr., in October. During the war, the Group flew 1,579 missions, destroyed 260 enemy planes, damaged 148 others, and sank
a German destroyer. Ninety-five of its pilots awarded
Distinguished Flying Cross.

Congress of Racial Equality (CORE) begins its career of protest in Chicago.

1943

Dr. James C. Evans becomes an official of U.S. War Department.

1944

In *Smith v. Allwright,* U.S. Supreme Court rules the all-white primary election unconstitutional.

In *Morgan v. Virginia,* U.S. Supreme Court reverses the conviction of a Negro passenger who violated Virginia's segregation laws by not vacating a bus seat, citing need for uniformity in the regulation of interstate commerce.

All-Negro 92nd Infantry Division loses 3,000 lives in Italian Campaign. Awarded 65 Silver Stars, 162 Bronze Stars, and 1,300 Purple Hearts.

1947

Armed forces unified and desegregated.

1948

President Truman appoints Dr. James C. Evans to supervise desegregation of the military establishment.

1950

In *McLaurin v. Board of Regents,* U.S. Supreme Court rules against classroom and social segregation of Negro student attending University of Oklahoma.

In *Sweat v. Painter,* U.S. Supreme Court rules that equality of education entails more than comparability of facilities, implying that "separate," by definition, must be unequal.

In *Henderson v. United States,* U.S. Supreme Court strikes down Interstate Commerce Commission ruling requiring Negro passengers in railroad dining cars to eat behind a partition.

Gwendolyn Brooks becomes only Negro woman to receive Pulitzer Prize, May 1.

Ralph J. Bunche becomes first Negro American to receive Nobel Peace Prize, September 22.

All-Negro 24th Infantry Regiment scores first victory of Korean conflict at Yechon, July 20.

1954

In *Brown v. Board of Education,* Supreme Court rules that "separate educational facilities are inherently unequal," striking down the ruling in *Plessy v. Ferguson.*

Washington, D. C., Wilmington, St. Louis, and Baltimore begin school desegregation.

1955

Interstate Commerce Commission orders the end of segregation in interstate travel.

Mrs. Rosa Parks refuses to vacate her bus seat, sparking the Negro boycott of Montgomery, Alabama bus system, December 1.

A. Phillip Randolph and Willard Townsend become vice presidents of the newly merged AFL-CIO.

1956

Seventy-seven Representatives and nineteen Senators issue "Southern Manifesto" questioning legality of the Supreme Court's ruling and defying its order to desegregate.

U.S. Supreme Court extends principles of Brown decision to higher education in ruling on *Florida, ex rel. Hawkins v. Board of Control.*

John H. Sengstacke launches *The Chicago Daily Defender,* one of the nation's two Negro daily newspapers.

Federal district court rules that segregation on public transportation violates both "due process" and "equal protection" provisions of the Fourteenth Amendment.

Montgomery, Alabama, desegregates its entire public transportation system, December.

1957

Congress passes Civil Rights Act of 1957, August 29. The 1957 Act establishes the United States Commission on Civil Rights as a temporary, independent, bipartisan agency. It also made provisions to protect and strengthen the voting rights of all American citizens.

Federal troops ordered to Little Rock, Arkansas, to facilitate desegregation of Central High School.

Dr. Martin Luther King and other Negro leaders form the Southern Christian Leadership Conference.

1958

Dr. Ralph J. Bunche becomes Under Secretary of the United Nations.

1960

President Eisenhower signs Civil Rights Act of 1960, May 6. The 1960 Act provides greater protection of voting rights and makes it a crime to damage property and transport or possess explosives for this purpose.

Founding of Student Non-Violent Coordinating Committee (SNCC or "SNICK").

1961

Robert C. Weaver appointed Administrator of the Housing and Home Finance Agency, February 11.

Clifton R. Wharton becomes U. S. ambassador to Norway, March 9.

James Benton Parsons becomes U.S. District Judge in Chicago, the first Negro appointed to a Federal District Court in *continental United States,* August 9.

Thurgood Marshall appointed to Second Circuit's Federal Court of Appeals, September 23.

Interstate Commerce Commission orders an end to segregated facilities in terminal buildings.

CORE Freedom Riders number over a thousand, white and Negro, in early part of the year.

1962

Negro and civil rights workers ask New York and Philadelphia to suspend building projects in which discrimination in hiring is evident. Such pleas, with demonstrations at construction sites, lead to some concessions in hiring and training.

1963

In one twelve-week period, 1,412 separate civil rights demonstrations take place.

Martin Luther King, Jr., leads demonstration in Birmingham, Alabama. Protest becomes violent, May 7, when Public Safety Commissioner "Bull" Connor orders fire hoses and dogs to be used against demonstrators.

NAACP Field Secretary, Medgar Evers, assassinated by segregationists, as he enters his home, June 12.

William Moore, Negro postal employee, shot to death as he staged a one-man "Freedom Walk."

More than a quarter million whites and Negroes stage a March on Washington for civil rights, August 28.

Four Negro girls killed in the bombing of their Birmingham, Alabama, Sunday School, September 15.

John Fitzgerald Kennedy, 35th President of the United States, assassinated in Dallas, Texas, November 22.

Carl Rowan appointed U.S. Ambassador to Norway.

1964

A series of apparently spontaneous riots break out in Northern cities. Among the worst, were those in the Harlem and Bedford-Stuyvesant sections of New York City; in Rochester, New York; Jersey City, New Jersey; Philadelphia, Pennsylvania; Dixmoor, Illinois.

Malcolm X announces his split with the Black Muslims and the founding of a new movement based on his theories of Black nationalism, March 12.

Bodies of three civil rights workers found in a crude grave near Philadelphia, Mississippi, August 4. The boys, two white and one Negro, were murdered by white segregationists, June 21.

Civil Rights Act, including public accommodations, voter registration and fair employment sections, signed into law by President Lyndon B. Johnson, July 2. Senate imposed cloture to end a Southern filibuster, June 10.

Dr. Martin Luther King, Jr., becomes second American Negro to win Nobel Peace Prize.

Carl Rowan appointed Director of the United States Information Agency.

Sidney Poiter becomes first Negro to win "Oscar" as best actor of the year, April 13.

1965

Constance Baker Motley is elected to the Manhattan Borough Presidency, the first woman to hold this post. Highest elective office ever held by a black woman.

In Atlanta, Paul L. Bellesen, a Negro Roman Catholic, who received a membership card from the Ku Klux Klan, has it revoked on February 25 by James R. Venable, head of the National Knights of the KKK. Venable had appointed Bellesen a Grand Titan, and asked him to organize a klavern in Bellesen's home state of Idaho.

Malcolm X is shot down, in New York, by three assassins and dies on the same day, February 21. His three murderers were convicted, March 11, 1966. Two of the three were members of the Black Muslim movement.

Several hundred Negroes attempt to march from Selma to Montgomery, Alabama, to protest withholding of Negro voter registration, Sunday, March 7, 1965. They are beaten back by state police with tear gas, bull whips, cattle prods and clubs.

On March 8, the U.S. Supreme Court, in a 9–0 decision, upholds the power of the Justice Department to sue a state to enforce Negro voting rights. This is in reference to a case in Mississippi.

Unitarian minister James Reeb, in Selma to participate in the march on Montgomery, is fatally beaten by four white men, March 9. He died two days later.

Addressing the nation in behalf of the Negro cause, President Johnson announces he will submit a voting rights bill to Congress, March 15.

Federal injunction granted, restraining officials from interfering in Selma march, March 17.

Freedom March from Selma to Montgomery, March 21.

White civil rights worker, Mrs. Viola Gregg Liuzzo, murdered by white segregationists, March 25.

Congress passes Voting Rights Act, August 4. It is signed by President Johnson, August 6. The 1965 Act provides new tools to assure the right to vote and supplements the previous authority granted by the Civil Rights Acts of 1957, 1960, and 1964.

Race riots break out in Watts area of Los Angeles, California. Riots last 7 days, from August 11 to August 17. Considered the most serious race riots in America's history.

Riots break out in a Chicago black ghetto from August 13 to 15; some 60 people are injured; over 2,000 national guardsmen are called in to restore order. Considered Chicago's worst riots in 13 years.

The McCone Commission delivers its report on the Watt's Riots, December 7. The Commission was set up by Governor Pat Brown of California.

Thurgood Marshall appointed Solicitor General of the United States.

Benjamin O. Davis gains rank of Lt. General in May and becomes Deputy Commander, U.S. Forces in Korea. Previously served as Director of Manpower and Training in USAF headquarters.

1966

Constance Baker Motley becomes first Negro woman to be appointed to a Judgeship in a Federal District Court. She is appointed Judge in Federal District Court of New York City, January 25.

Anti-Defamation League of the B'nai B'rith charges the John Birch Society with "waging all out war against the Civil Rights Movement," primarily by influencing "voting rights at local level." January 31.

James Farmer leaves his post as Director of CORE. Takes position of leadership in the newly formed National Center for Community Action and Education, Inc., February.

Robert C. Weaver becomes first Negro cabinet member. He is appointed by President Johnson head of the newly created Department of Housing and Urban Development, January 17.

Two Negro senators and nine Negro congressmen elected to the Georgia legislature.

Stokely Carmichael takes over leadership of Student Non-Violent Coordinating Committee (SNCC), and announces policy of "black power," a political and economic movement calling for removal of whites from leadership and policy-making positions within the civil rights organizations.

Floyd McKissick, a North Carolina lawyer, becomes National Director of the Congress of Racial Equality (CORE). CORE subsequently joins SNCC in the espousal of "black power," and both organizations modify their traditional commitments to "non-violence."

Robert C. Henry elected mayor of Springfield, Ohio. He was the first Negro to be chief executive of a Northern city, or of any American city of substantial size.

Lucius A. Amerson elected sheriff of Macon County (Tuskegee), Alabama. He was the first Negro to be elected sheriff in the history of the United States.

Georgia Legislature refuses to seat Julian Bond because of his stand on Vietnam, February 10.

New riot in Watts area of Los Angeles kills two, injures at least 25. Hundreds of black youths involved. 200 police restore order. March 15.

The U.S. Supreme Court outlaws the poll tax for all elections on March 25.

The first Negro Arts Festival is held in Dakar, Senegal, from April 1–24.

White House Conference on Civil Rights attended by 2,000 participants, June 1–20.

James Meredith is shot from ambush on June 6 shortly after beginning a 220 mile voting rights pilgrimage from Memphis, Tennessee, to Jackson, Mississippi.

The march begun by James Meredith ends in front of the state capitol in Jackson. Addresses by Meredith, Martin Luther King and Stokely Carmichael who urges the 15,000 blacks in attendance to "build a base of power." June 26.

The National Convention of the Congress of Racial Equality votes to adopt a resolution endorsing the concept of "black power" as enunciated by Stokely Carmichael during the Meredith march, July 1–4.

The NAACP disassociates itself from the "black power" doctrine, July 4–9. Vice-president Humphrey supports their position.

Three nights of rioting on Chicago's west side—National Guard is called in to restore order, July 15.

Riots take place in Chicago Negro ghetto; last four days; 5,000 blacks, many armed, fight police; 4,000 guardsmen called in to quell fighting; 2 dead, scores wounded. July 13–16.

Rioting in Hough, Cleveland; 4 killed, 50 injured and 164 arrests, July 18–23.

Racial violence in Omaha, Atlanta, and Minneapolis on August 3.

Martin Luther King, Jr., is stoned in Chicago on August 5. Near-rioting. 4,000 whites and 960 policemen.

Southern Regional Council reports on August 5 that voter registration in six Southern states has risen from 30% to 46% of eligible Negroes since passage of Voting Rights Act.

CORE holds "black power" rally in Harlem, attended by McKissick; Baba Oseijeman, self-styled "Prime Minister of Harlem Peoples' Parliament;" Livingston Wingate and some black nationalist leaders. Cambodian representative to the U.S., Huot Sambath, also attends. McKissick hails six elements of "black power;" late Malcolm X hailed. August 15.

900 Ohio National Guardsmen with several policemen and sheriff's deputies patrol Dayton streets after Negroes riot in West Side area following fatal shooting of Negro by white, September 2.

In Atlanta, Georgia, police use tear gas and fire shotguns in air to disperse over 400 Negroes, including 10 SNCC members, rioting to protest police shooting of Negro robbery suspect; SNCC chairman Stokely Carmichael had told Negroes to "tear this place up." White officials and state politicians blame SNCC for riot. Carmichael arrested and charged with inciting to riot. September 8.

National Guardsmen are called to quell racial rioting in south-eastern San Francisco, September 28.

1967

Edward Brooke elected U. S. Senator from Massachusetts. First black senator since Reconstruction.

Lester Maddox, militant segregationist, elected governor of Georgia by a vote of 182–66 in state legislature, January 10.

House of Representatives excludes Adam Clayton Powell from his seat in Congress on March 1. Grounds were misuse of public funds and Powell's defiance of a New York court order to pay a court judgment.

Adam Clayton Powell re-elected to House of Representatives from Harlem in a special election, April 11.

National Guardsmen take over Jackson State College campus in wake of racial disorder, May 11.

Stokely Carmichael resigns as chairman of SNCC and H. Rap Brown becomes new chairman, May 12.

Supreme Court in 9–0 decision, rules that states constitutionally can't bar inter-racial marriages, June 12.

Thurgood Marshall named Associate Justice of the U.S. Supreme Court, June 13.

National Guard helps end racial violence in Cincinnati, Ohio, June 15.

In Houston, Cassius Clay, deposed heavy-weight champion of boxing, found guilty of draft refusal; sentenced to 5 years in prison, and fined $10,000, June 20.

Buffalo, New York, blacks battle police as riots break out for second time in 24 hours, June 28.

Newark riots break out; started by protest over rumors that a black taxi driver had been killed in a scuffle with police. 26 killed; 1,500 reported injured; damage estimates vary from $10 to 30 million. July 12–17.

National Guard troops move into Minneapolis after two days of rioting, July 21.

Major riots break out in Detroit. Cause thought to be reaction to police raids on black private social clubs. 2,700 army troops are called in to restore law and order. Over 40 dead; over 2,000 injured; property damage from $250–500 million, July 22–27.

President Johnson appoints a special commission headed by Governor Otto Kerner of Illinois to investigate riots. July 27.

Stokely Carmichael in a speech in Havana on August 17 calls for "total revolution" in U.S.

Five days of disorder in New Haven, Connecticut, come to an end, August 23.

President names Walter E. Washington to be first commissioner of Washington, D.C., on September 6. He becomes first black chief executive of a major city.

Carl B. Stokes and Richard G. Hatcher elected mayors of Cleveland and Gary (Indiana). Blacks elected to the state legislatures in Virginia, Mississippi and Louisiana for the first time since Reconstruction, November 8.

1968

Black congressmen hold office in 24 state legislatures. 12 states have black senators. Black mayors head 8 city governments.

Julian Bond of Atlanta nominated for president at the Democratic National Convention, meeting in Chicago.

Seven Blackamericans hold ambassadorial appointments under President Lyndon Baines Johnson: Elliot Skinner, Mercer Cook, Mrs. Patricia Harris, Clinton Knox, James Nabrit, Hugh Smythe and Franklin Williams.

Racial violence in Orangeburg, South Carolina. Three Black students killed and forty wounded by police and National Guard gun fire, February 7–8.

Report of the National Advisory Commission on Civil Disorders, headed by Otto Kerner, is released on March 1. It states that the nation is heading toward two societies—one black, one white, separate and unequal. Further states that root cause of disorders is white institutional racism, and that further riots can only be prevented by massive government (local, state and particularly federal) aid.

Martin Luther King, Jr., president of the Southern Christian Leadership Conference, Nobel Peace Laureate, and apostle of non-violent tactics for social change, is assassinated in Memphis, Tennessee, April 4. Reverend Ralph Abernathy succeeds King as president of SCLC.

The rioting which followed Dr. King's death claimed at least 39 dead (later revised to 46); more than 3,500 injured, including 1,166 in Washington, 1,000 in Chicago and 900 in Baltimore. Over 20,000 arrests made. 125 cities in 29 states and the District of Columbia hit. Property damage over $45,000,000. 68,887 troops used, including 21,586 U.S. army troops.

Racial violence in Louisville, May 27.

Presidential aspirant and friend of the black man, Senator Robert F. Kennedy, assassinated in Los Angeles. Assassin, Sirhan Sirhan, apprehended, June 5.

Two black men charged with plotting to kill Roy Wilkins and Whitney B. Young, June 15.

50,000 people join in a freedom march in support of the Poor People's campaign in Washington, June 19.

James Baldwin, noted black writer, speaks before the World Council of Churches' convention in Geneva, and indicts the Christian Church for its lack of support and concern for the plight of the black man, July 7.

Democratic National Convention, August 26–29. 218 black delegates and 180 black alternates. Mississippi's Free Democrats replace regular Democrats. Half of Julian Bond's Georgia delegation is seated. Other challenges are defeated. Reverend Channing Phillips is nominated for President and receives 67½ votes.

Black power protest at the Olympics in Mexico City when Tommy Smith and John Carlos raise clinched black gloved fists to protest racism in America, October 16.

Black students' union seizes two floors of administration building at San Francisco State University, November 4.

Richard Nixon is elected President. Many black candidates are elected to office across the country, but "black vote" is against Nixon. November 5.

1969

T.V. DISCOVERS THE BLACKAMERICANS: JULIA, first series to star black woman; COWBOY IN AFRICA features little Gerald Edwards; MISSION IMPOSSIBLE shows Greg Morris; LAND OF GIANTS shows newcomer Don Marshall. STAR TREK features Michelle Nichols as communications operator on spaceship; PEYTON PLACE adds black family to cast. Percy Rodriques is husband of Ruby Dee. Gynn Turman plays their teenage son. Other black men in prominent roles are Clarence Williams (*Mod Squad.*), Hari Rodes (*Daktari*), Ivan Dixon (*Hogan's Heroes*), Don Mitchell (*Ironside*), Gail Foster (*Mannix*), Mail Goode is ABC news correspondent at U.N., Bill Matney is NBC news correspondent in Chicago, George Foster host of Black America, Bob Teague covers for NBC in New York. Film Star—Jim Brown.

Mrs. Shirley Chisholm is first black woman in Congress. Louis Stokes, 43, the first black Congressman from Cleveland, Ohio. William Caly, 36, the first black man to represent Missouri on Capitol Hill.

Harris Lewis of New Meadow, New York, and Willie Bussel were two of the U.S.S. *Pueblo*'s black men who spent 335 days as captives by the North Koreans.

One Year Later, a follow-up to the Kerner report confirms that the direction of the U.S. is still toward two societies, separate and unequal, March 6.

Sgt. Rodney M. Davis of Macon, Georgia, is awarded the Medal of Honor for Heroism in Vietnam. He is the tenth Blackamerican to receive the award for service in Vietnam, and the 47th black in U.S. military history to be honored with the nation's highest citation. The award is posthumous. March 26.

The Black Academy of Arts and Letters is founded in New York with a select membership of "those who have made a notable impact upon the arts, letters and culture of black people." The fifty founders include John Hope Franklin, Ossie Davis, John O. Killens, Duke Ellington, and Charles White. C. Eric Lincoln elected founding President. March 27.

Index